PROGRAM READY

23
QUICK AND COMPLETE PROGRAMS
FOR THE CHURCH YEAR

PROGRAM READY

23
QUICK AND COMPLETE PROGRAMS
FOR THE CHURCH YEAR

DOROTHY MacNEILL

THE UNITED CHURCH PUBLISHING HOUSE

Program Ready
23 Quick and Complete Programs for the Church Year
Copyright © The United Church Publishing House

The Christmas Candle-Lighting Service first appeared in *Quick 'N' Easy* as "Mary Christmas" and the Advent Carols first appeared in *Quick'N'Easy Number Two*, both self-published by Dorothy MacNeill.

Canadian Cataloguing in Publication Data
MacNeill, Dorothy, 1934-
    Program ready : 23 quick and complete programs for the church year

Includes bibliographical references and index.

ISBN 1-55134-037-2

1. Worship programs. 2. Church year. I. Title.

BV198.M35 1994   264   C94-931895-7

The United Church Publishing House
85 St. Clair Avenue East
Toronto, Ontario
M4T 1M8

Project Editor: J. Elizabeth Gillan Muir
Managing Editor: Ruth Bradley-St-Cyr
Book Design: Dept. of Graphics and Print
Cover Design: Gordon Szendrey
Printed in Canada by: Kromar Printing Ltd.

1 2 3 4 5   98 97 96 95 94

CONTENTS

PREFACE

Dorothy MacNeill has done it again! Following on the success of her first two self-published books, *Quick'N'Easy* and *Quick'N'Easy Number Two*, this third collection of "user-friendly" programs, *Program Ready*, is the most extensive yet. Based on the church year, the sessions guide the user through the various seasons and church celebrations—Thanksgiving, Advent, Christmas, Lent, Easter, and Pentecost.

Program leaders with little time to prepare will welcome the format of worship and discussion segments, each complete in itself. To accomodate varying needs, flexibility is built in so that each session can be easily adapted to different situations and used by a wide variety of groups and ages. Included are a drama and other ideas for Christmas, units that explore our most basic emotions such as joy and loneliness, and a number of programs based on women in the Bible.

The discussion questions are both topical and incisive. MacNeill has a talent for zeroing in on the everyday and the commonplace, allowing the participants to relate to familiar situations. At the same time we are encouraged to explore new ways of thinking and to examine new ideas.

Groups and individuals who have found the author's earlier self-published books so helpful will be eager to explore this new offering. It is my hope that many others will take advantage of her extensive gifts in developing resource material that is easy to use, stimulating, and exciting.

Elizabeth Gillan Muir, Editor
Stewardship Education Officer
The United Church of Canada

ACKNOWLEDGEMENTS

Thanks, first and foremost, to Elizabeth Gillan Muir for editing the material.

Grateful acknowledgement is made for permission to use the following material:
- "Symbol of Hope," copyright Betty Turcott. Permission to reprint words and music for one-time use is graciously granted.
- "A Place For You," copyright Division of Mission in Canada, The United Church of Canada. Permission to reprint a section of the report is granted.

Unless otherwise marked, scripture quotations are from the *New Revised Standard Version* of the Bible. KJV refers to the *King James Version* of the Bible

Hymn resources have been chosen from two sources. The titles of these works have been abbreviated as follows:

HB   *The Hymn Book of the Anglican Church of Canada and the United Church of Canada* (1971).

SGP   *Songs for a Gospel People* (Wood Lake Books, 1988).

The Hymnary refers to *The Hymnary of the United Church of Canada*, (The United Church Publishing House, 1930).

INTRODUCTION

With the increased use of the Common Lectionary there are many congregations for whom the seasons of the church year are becoming as much a part of their lives as the changing seasons of the natural year. The use of colour and banners in our churches serves to emphasize the different seasons. Such activities have proven invaluable as teaching tools for our children and have provided opportunities for families to enrich traditional celebrations.

The programs in this book start with a period of "ordinary time," since September is the unofficial beginning of the church year. This time period is sometimes called the season of Creation. The programs conclude with another period of "ordinary time," between Pentecost and September. Many groups do not meet during the summer but these, or any of the programs, may be used at any time. Each program has a short devotional section and suggestions for group discussion. These programs were originally written for use in church women's groups, but they are easily adaptable for use with mixed adult groups, or with young people. The length of time required for presentation will depend on the size of your group and the interest in the topic, but there should be ample material for at least thirty minutes.

Although the contents of this book are "program ready," I hope they will also stimulate you to develop programs of your own around topics of particular interest to your group. "Starting from Scratch" provides a few organizational and creative tips to help you get started. No written material is general enough to suit every situation; adaptation and improvisation are encouraged. Your own creativity can always enhance the printed word.

It is impossible to thank everyone who has helped me with this material, or to name the books or people whose ideas have become integrated with my own. We are all made up of the bits and pieces of others that rub off on us through our various relationships and experiences. I hope that bits and pieces of these programs will become a part of you, my reader. For me, that is the best reason of all for sharing them.

Dorothy MacNeill
Woodstock, New Brunswick
1994

Dedicated to
a good friend, Rilla McLean,
who lives as though
her crutches are wings.

Fall

Fall

Priscilla, Superwoman Model

WORSHIP

Call to Worship
Perfectionists refuse or delay doing things unless they can be done to perfection. If we waited until we were worthy to come into the presence of God we would not offer God our worship and praise. We believe, however, that God understands our reluctance, and welcomes the feeble response of our hearts. Let us worship God.

Prayer
We remember, O God, the simple prayers taught to us in our childhood. We regret that sometimes those are the words that still spring to our lips when we seek your presence or ask your favour. Help us to grow in our faith, to find new and better ways of sharing our thoughts and concerns with you, for we believe you care. We *know* that you care, because you gifted us with your son, Jesus, in whose name we pray. Amen.

Hymn

"God Who Touchest Earth with Beauty" (#243 HB)

Scripture

Acts 18:24-28

Reflection

Priscilla and her husband Aquila are mentioned five times in the New Testament. Three times Priscilla's name comes before her husband's, and yet when one looks up "Priscilla" in *Cruden's Concordance* the reference is to "see Aquila."[1] How reluctant the church has been to recognize and celebrate the contributions of women of faith.

Priscilla (also referred to as Prisca, a diminutive of her name) was quite a woman. Maybe the original Superwoman! Studious and practical, and very influential. In the story we just heard we note that Priscilla was also something of a perfectionist. It didn't matter that Apollos was eloquent and familiar with the scriptures. He didn't have the story quite right, so Priscilla and Aquila "took him aside and explained the Way of God to him more accurately." (Acts 18:26b) Is it not easy to believe that the tents Priscilla made were of excellent quality, and the hospitality she extended to numerous guests a model of perfection?

Priscilla could be a role model for the modern woman who wishes to combine a career with both homemaking and study. As well as her other duties, an early church congregation met in her house. She did it all. She was also a very courageous woman, and the tribute paid to her by Paul in his letter to the Romans implies that Priscilla was a prominent female leader at a time when Christians were being persecuted. In Romans 16:3 we read, "Greet Prisca and Aquila, who work with me in Christ Jesus, and who *risked their necks* for my life, to whom not only I give thanks, but also all the churches of the Gentiles. Greet also the church in their house."

In her book *All of the Women of the Bible*,[2] Edith Deen suggests that Priscilla was influenced by Paul's words in the book of Hebrews, Chapter 13, verses 20 and 21. In the *King James Version* this reads, in part, "May the God of peace ... make you *perfect* in every good work..." It is interesting to note that this has been altered in the *New Revised Standard Version* of the Bible. Here we read "Now may the God of peace ... make you *complete* in everything good..." Could this be why generations of women have sought perfection instead of completeness?

Prayer

We wish we had that perfect commitment to your will, O God. The desire to work, to relax, to relate well to family and friends, and also to study and prepare ourselves for service in your church. Have patience with us, O God, for we know that you are not finished with us yet. Help us to understand that as we seek to become fully human, to be complete and in harmony with our surroundings and with you, we are living our lives according to your will and purpose. Amen.

PROGRAM

If you are in a room where things can be attached to the walls without causing damage, make a few posters such as the following:

- Dull people have immaculate houses
- They finally found something to do the work of five men — one woman!
- If you want something done, ask a busy woman
- Kitchen closed because of illness — Mother is sick of cooking

After these have been put on the walls, or held up, discuss why we find them funny. What truths do they hide?

Sometimes when one member of an organization is very capable and efficient, there is a reluctance on the part of other people to actively participate or offer their leadership skills. Strong leaders can intimidate without realizing it. How can we reinforce the fact that every group needs the support and participation of *all* of its members?

Discuss the difference between being "perfect" and being "complete." The dictionary is not much help, because it says that they are basically the same. Have you ever heard anyone criticized for being a completionist? Why is a perfectionist often viewed in a negative way?

To close, list some characteristics of a "complete" woman and contrast those with ideas about the "perfect" woman.

Suggested Reading
Gift from the Sea, by Anne Morrow Lindbergh. Written over thirty years ago, this book has become a timeless classic and should be required reading for anyone who wants to find balance in life and a quiet space for contemplation.

Mahala, the Ordinary

WORSHIP

Call to Worship

Not many "ordinary" people will have their names recorded in the history books yet unwritten. Some of us will live and die without seeing our name or picture in the local newspaper. Many men and women will not be listed as a member of some committee or organization. Some will be without a friend to hold their hand as they grow old. Let us worship our God, who knows all of us by name, and who loves each one of us dearly.

Prayer

Help us, O God, to offer this prayer for people whom the world considers insignificant. Some of them are us. Many we do not know by name. They are living ordinary lives, eating, sleeping, working. They do not look for recognition. Many enjoy their invisibility. We pray that they may recognize that you are present with them, at all times. We celebrate those who have done or are doing great things in this world, but help us to also celebrate those who do the ordinary things of life. In Jesus name, Amen.

Hymn

"Help Us Accept Each Other" (#8 SGP)

Scripture

1 Chronicles 7:18 and Psalm 8:1-9 (*New Revised Standard Version*, if possible)

REFLECTION

The first chapters of 1 Chronicles are filled with genealogical records, names that are strange to our eyes and ears. There are forty-two women named, many of whom appear nowhere else in the Bible. They may have been listed because of the importance of their husbands, or the children they bore. Mahala (or Mahlah) was one of three children born to Gilead's sister Hammolecheth. Gilead belonged to the family of Joseph, definitely an important family.

A woman named Mahala Brace lived in a small outport in Newfoundland during the late 1800's. She was a very ordinary person. No one ever noted or remembered why she was named after this obscure woman in 1 Chronicles. Biblical names were given to children simply because they were found in the Bible, which had been the major source of names for generations. This Mahala was married to a fisherman. They lived in a very small house, without running water or electricity, with their three children. When the youngest child was barely three years old Mahala's husband was lost at sea.

As a widow, she was completely dependent on the community. Other fishermen would bring her fish; the local merchant would see that she had some flour and sugar and tea. No doubt she would pay for these things through baby-sitting, or housecleaning. She planted a few potatoes and turnips in the sparse topsoil of the seaside village. She carried water, and emptied chamber pots. She baked bread in a tiny stove, kept the floor scrubbed clean and made patchwork quilts for the beds.

Mahala's children grew. The oldest child, Gertrude, moved away to be a live-in servant for a family moving to the United States. At age nine the middle child, Minnie, worked for the local merchant's wife. At fourteen she left home to "go into service" in another community. By the time Minnie was twenty she was a maid in a very fashionable house in the city. At twenty-eight she married a young plumber, who eventually became a successful contractor. They would take their children to visit Mahala, but they could never persuade her to leave her home.

With her children grown and a son who stayed at home, life became easier for Mahala, even though her son's first wife died after her third child, and the second marriage was not a happy one. Mahala died in the same small house where she lived all her married life. She was a very ordinary person who considered raising three children alone something that was simply required of her, something which she did with the support of God and her community. This is probably the first time her name has ever appeared in print.[3]

Prayer

Thank you God for the heritage that is ours through parents and grandparents. Thank you also for our greater heritage, for we are inheritors of the faith of all who have ever called themselves "Christian." Surrounded by this mighty cloud of witnesses, may we live our lives so that those who follow us will cherish the stories told of ordinary people, those who sought only to seek justice, love mercy, and walk humbly with you, their God. Amen.

PROGRAM

Many people can tell stories about their names. Take a few moments for group members to share why they have the name they use, whom they were "called after" or any other interesting aspect of their given name. If you have a book of names and if your group is small you may wish to share the meaning of the names of the people present.

The 8th Psalm marvels that God, who created such a wonderful universe, should yet care for humans. Have people share experiences when they felt awed by the wonder of God's creation and were amazed at our place in it.

The Psalmist asks, "what are *human beings* that you are mindful of them, *mortals* that you care for them?" (Psalm 8:4) Discuss the implications of this in terms of people who make the front pages of our newspapers and those who are homeless. What about those who hold leadership positions and those who simply come to our meetings, or attend our Sunday worship? If God is mindful and cares for *all* humans, are we called do the same? Is it *possible* for us to care for all the people in the world? Do we set boundaries on our caring to avoid "compassion fatigue"? Are there other ways to avoid becoming overwhelmed by the immensity of the task to love and care for one another?

Suggest to members that they reach out to someone during the coming week, someone they would not normally see or contact, just to say "Hello — how are you?" — and mean it!

Living Thanks

WORSHIP

Call to Worship
Come before God with thanksgiving. Give thanks unto the Lord — We are bound to thank God — Offer a sacrifice of thanks. The Bible never lets us forget the necessity of giving thanks.

Prayer
Yes, God, we're all thankful, but... sometimes we have to confess that we would be a little more thankful if our house were a little bigger, our debts were a little smaller, or if we received a little more appreciation. We're thankful, but it would be so nice to be younger, prettier, thinner, richer. Forgive us, O God. Create within us clean hearts, so that we can be thankful without any strings attached. Amen.

Hymn
"For the Fruit of All Creation" (#58 SGP) or "Come Ye Thankful People, Come" (#384 HB)

Scripture
   Luke 17:11-19

REFLECTION

You may have thought the opening prayer for this worship service was a bit disrespectful. It wasn't meant to be. It was to help us realize that in our daily lives we often hear more grumbling about what people *want*, than expressions of thanksgiving for what they *have*. As polite Christians, we can easily list all the things for which we *could* be thankful — our health, our free country, our families, friends, and neighbours. And then there are the traditional things for which we usually express thanks at this time of year — a good harvest, lots of food for our tables, and the fellowship we enjoy in our congregation.

In spite of this, it isn't difficult to detect an undercurrent of envy in some voices we hear at work, in the supermarket, or maybe even at coffee after church: "Did you know that Joe Jones won the Lotto? Lucky man!" "Rosa and Don are going to Hawaii this March — don't I wish *we* could go!" "Saw a beautiful dress this week, just can't afford it, though" or even, "He's so lucky to be thin — and he eats everything in sight."

Envy is one of the deadly sins. It is expressly forbidden in the Ten Commandments. There the word used is *covet* and there is a long list of things which we are not to covet. That is to say, we are told not to want anything that someone else has. That doesn't mean that we shouldn't admire what other people have, and it doesn't prevent us from obtaining something similar for ourselves. But, to paraphrase the Serenity Prayer,[4] we would like to pray, "God grant us all of what we need, some of what we want, and the wisdom to know the difference."

At Thanksgiving time we can use the opportunity to lay aside all envy and malice, to be heartily thankful for *that which we have*. Period. We can list our blessings, with no "buts," no "if onlys," no "after Christmas," or "when my ship comes in."

We can be thankful *now*. All of us are alive today. That in itself is cause for thanksgiving. Today and every day.

Story p. 76. The Thoughtful Are Thankful.

Prayer

For two things especially we give thanks to you, Almighty God. We thank you for life itself, and we thank you for the life of your son, Jesus. Help us to give evidence of the thanksgiving in our hearts by living in a thankful way. Amen.

Service Book 351

PROGRAM

Allow people time to react to the thoughts expressed during worship. Give people the opportunity to disagree or elaborate.

Thanksgiving is a good time to think of an outreach program. You may want to invite someone from a local food bank to speak to your group, and then have the group make some effort to contribute, either as a group or as a congregation.

Or, you might think ahead to Christmas and develop an idea that would enlarge your usual Christmas projects. For example, one women's group photocopied outlines of turkeys, cut them out, fastened them to a poster which said — "Enjoy your Christmas Dinner twice as much, by providing a turkey for a needy family this year." People who wished to contribute took a turkey cutout, gave the money to a designated person, so that receipts could be issued. The money was used by the local food bank to purchase turkeys for their clients.

Alternate Program

Have everyone print their first name on a small piece of paper. Place the papers in a bowl, and then have everyone draw one out. (Replace and draw again if you get your own name.)

Think about the person whose name is on your slip of paper. Write below the name, "I am thankful that you belong to this group because ..."

Allow the group adequate time to complete the sentence. Put the papers back into the bowl, draw them again, and read them aloud. Now people will be reading about other persons present, reading things like "Mary Smith, I am thankful that you belong to this group because you always manage to make us laugh." or "Mei-ling Chan, I am thankful that you belong to this group because you understand the Bible so well."

If there is still discussion time available, divide the large group into smaller groups to share their earliest memories of Thanksgiving.

Close by asking everyone to share one thing for which they are particularly thankful.

Advent, Christmas, and Epiphany

Advent Expectations

WORSHIP *Vere:*

Call to Worship
Prepare the way, we're expecting Good News! Getting ready for the birth of Christ seems almost simple — compared to getting ready for the Christmas festivities that overshadow our lives during the Advent season. Advent means "waiting." In words that may seem old fashioned, let us "wait" upon the Lord.

Prayer
In this quiet time, O God, we await the awareness of your presence with us. We bring many expectations into the Advent and Christmas season. Expectations of joyful gatherings of family and friends, surprises and warm greetings. As we prepare for another celebration of the birth of your son, help us to make our expectations realistic, our goals achievable. Above all, let us expect to feel even closer to you during these Advent days of preparation. Amen.

Explanation of Advent — the season of advent In our church year the 4 weeks or Sundays preceding Christmas Day, the day we celebrate Christ's coming Advent is a interesting word. The dictionary refers to it as an important arrival, an adventure is an unusual & exciting experience. Advent is a time of waiting, of expectation and of preparation. and so we wait and prepare to experience this important event,

Hymn

"When John the Baptist Did Proclaim" or "Advent Season Gives the Reason" (both found in the resource section of this book) or "There's a Voice in the Wilderness" (#153, HB)

Scripture

Luke 1:26-38

REFLECTION

We always seem to get a little mixed up in Advent. The stores in our communities have already put up their Christmas decorations, Christmas parties are in full swing, and it seems as though our Christmas celebrations are over almost before the day has come and gone. Preparing our hearts for the coming of the Christ Child in such a busy month is difficult indeed.

We may not be able to change the way our current culture rushes the Christmas season, but we can certainly find some time in the weeks before Christmas to do some prayerful and thoughtful planning ourselves.

One of the things we could do is to take an honest look at our *expectations* of Christmas. Many people are depressed and disappointed with Christmas because their expectations for the day are much too high, and often completely unrealistic. If our friends and relatives are in the same income bracket as ourselves we cannot expect one of them to give us a new car or a cruise to Jamaica for a Christmas present.

We may not think that we expect large gifts, but it isn't difficult to find a sense of disappointment around the Christmas tree when the gifts are opened. We are subconsciously wishing for the perfect gift — the gift that will convince us that we are truly loved.

If we can tune out this expectation, we can learn to recognize the love that comes with the most seemingly insignificant gift or in a smile, a greeting or an action that becomes a gift in itself.

Another unrealistic expectation is that Christmas will somehow be a different kind of day. We hope that the children won't fight, or that our spouse will not spend the day watching TV. We hope that Aunt Milly doesn't tell the same stories that she tells every Christmas. Women are the ones who tend to feel guilty if these great expectations aren't met. We feel that if we had been "nicer" to everyone, or if we had done more preparation, the day would have been as perfect as we wanted it to be. To avoid self blame when things don't turn out just right, we need to remind ourselves that family and friends will probably not change for this one day. *During this advent season let each of us reflect on what our expectations are.*

Prayer

Save us from our good intentions, we pray O God, and make our expectations more realistic. Help us to relax and allow Christmas to happen as it will. Remind us of the real reason for our celebrations and help us to include some outreach to the lonely and sick and old, and those who find the season difficult or unbearable. Amen.

PROGRAM

Divide into groups if there are sufficient numbers or assign the following names to individuals:

- Mary
- Joseph
- Elizabeth
- Zachariah

- Herod
- The Wise Men
- The Shepherds

Ask each group or person to check the first chapters of the gospels and read about the character or characters they have been assigned. (You may feel it necessary to have a concordance available. A good opportunity to demonstrate its use.) Then answer this question: What did this person, or these people, expect from Jesus? If you can't find an actual answer in the Bible story, use your imagination. What do you *think* they were looking for?

Share the answers and discuss the differences between the expectations of the people involved in the story and *our* expectations, almost two thousand years later.

Consider this: The Jewish people have always looked forward to the coming of one who would save them, a Messiah. They did not accept Jesus as this promised one, so they still live in a state of hope. It has sustained them through a very difficult history. Do Christians have a similar hope, in spite of our belief that Jesus was the Messiah foretold by the prophets?

Close by asking everyone to share what they expect from the coming Christmas celebrations.

Christmas Memories

Most Christmas programs in church groups take the form of a party. The following material could enrich a Christmas party by allowing a time for worship and a time for sharing without detracting from the festive feeling of your celebrations.

WORSHIP

Call to Worship
This is a festive time, a time to celebrate the season of our Saviour's birth. Let us sing together the first verse of the hymn, "Lord of the Dance" (#106 HB). (As an alternative to singing, read the first verse aloud as your Call to Worship.)

Prayer
Dance with us now, O God, as we pause before our party time to acknowledge your presence with us and to praise and thank you for the gift of your son, Jesus. We are happy here, taking this time away from our busy Christmas preparations and sharing our Christmas memories. We believe that our need to celebrate is one of the most enjoyable parts of your plan and purpose for your

people, and we thank you for it. Accept our celebrations as you accept our worship and our work. Amen.

Hymn
  Carol singing, as desired

Scripture
  Luke 2:8-15

REFLECTION

Glory to God in the highest! Shout for joy! Dance wherever you may be! Christmas is a time of joy and dancing and we are here to celebrate the birth of God's child.

As we move closer to the year 2000, it is interesting to speculate which Christmas will be more exciting — December 25, 1999, as we edge our way into another century, or December 25, 2000, which would be, according to our calendar, the 2000th birthday of Jesus of Nazareth. Pause for a minute, and consider that the birthday of one child, the life of one person, could be so powerful as to influence 2000 years of history.

Let your mind drift back, now, close your eyes and be as one of the shepherds on the hillside above Bethlehem. Imagine, if you can, the cold dark night, the quietness, and then the impact of angel voices "... Glory to God in the highest ..." (Pause)

Think about the youngest baby you have ever held. It may have been your own child, a niece or nephew, or an infant in a neonatal unit of your local hospital. How did you feel? (Pause)

Can you imagine how Mary may have felt, so young and having her baby in a strange town, in such humble surroundings? (Pause)

It is said that Mary *pondered* these things in her heart. She was storing up memories of Jesus the baby that she would later be able to share with those who knew Jesus as an adult. How thankful we are that Luke decided to include these stories in his gospel narrative.

Hymn
"While Shepherds Watched their Flocks by Night" (#405 HB)

PROGRAM

In preparation, wrap a small gift in six layers of plain white paper. Add a ribbon to make it look more festive. Write one of the following instructions on each of the wrappings:

First wrap: Share your earliest memory of Christmas

Second wrap: Share your funniest memory of Christmas

Third wrap: Is there a Christmas gift that you will never forget?

Fourth wrap: Is there a Christmas Day that you will never forget?

Fifth wrap: What is your favourite Christmas food. Why?

Sixth wrap: Does your family have any unique Christmas traditions?

As leader, remove the ribbon and throw (or pass) the gift to another member of the group. This person unwraps it and follows the instructions on the paper. After the memory is shared the gift is thrown to someone else, who unwraps another layer and follows the next instruction. Continue until someone receives the actual gift.

If you group is small, and/or if you wish to spend more time on the program part of your Christmas party, you could encourage others to add their memories to the one shared by the person unwrapping the gift. Or the last question could be answered by any and all who wish to share their unique traditions.

Enjoy your Christmas party — maybe it will become one of your best Christmas memories.

Christmas Candle-Lighting

This Candle-Lighting service can be used in a church sanctuary, church parlour, or a living-room. Costumes could be used, but are not necessary. You will need copies of the script for each person taking part, hymn books and music, and three candles (one blue, one brown and one white.) If you wish to have individual candles you will need one for each person expected. Circles of cardboard to form a protective collar will prevent wax from dripping.

WORSHIP

Call to Worship
The Word became a human being and, full of grace and truth, lived among us. The gospel says that other humans saw the glory of the one who was born a child. May we catch a glimpse of that glory now as we worship together.

Prayer

Hear our prayer, O God. Help us to see the glory which Jesus received as your only Son. Help us to feel a Christmas spirit in our hearts, a spirit which moves beyond the beauty of candles and trees, beyond an abundance of good cheer, into the very heart of the greatest gift our world has ever received. In Jesus' name we pray. Amen.

Hymn

"O Come All Ye Faithful" (#415 HB)

REFLECTION

Narrator: In our love and adoration of the baby Jesus, we sometimes forget the centrality of Mary, the mother of Jesus, in the Christmas story. We cannot possibly understand how Mary felt when the angel spoke to her. Some of us don't even believe in angels! But we have all dreamed dreams, we have all had experiences that cannot be explained. Listen, then, to what Mary *might* have said to the angel.

Mary: Oh, you startled me. What strange clothing you are wearing — do you live around here?

Angel: *No, Mary. I am not of this world at all. I am an angel.*

Mary: An angel! I've heard of angels, but I never expected to see one. Why have you come? Why have you come to see *me?*

Angel: *Angels are messengers, Mary, and I have a very important message for you.*

Mary: A message? From who? Are you sure you have the right person?

Angel: *The message is from God, Mary. Surely you know that angels are God's messengers.*

Mary: Yes, I suppose I do know that. But what message, and why me?

Angel: *The message is that you have been chosen to be the mother of a very special baby. God's very own child, actually.*

Mary: Me? A baby? But I'm not married. And as far as having God's baby, that's just a little hard to believe.

Angel: *I know it's hard to believe, Mary. But it's true. I hope you're going to cooperate in this.*

Mary: Do I have any choice? I've always tried to be the kind of girl that I thought God wanted me to be, but I never dreamed that God would ask me to do something like this! And how am I supposed to explain this to Joseph?

Angel: *Joseph will receive a message too, Mary, and he will accept this child as his own.*

Narrator: The language is not biblical, but the message is clear — Mary knows that she has been chosen by God for a very special task. Listen again, as she speaks to Joseph, her husband-to-be.

Mary: Joseph, could I talk to you a minute, please?

Joseph:	*Of course, Mary, what is it?*
Mary:	Well... I think I'm pregnant.
Joseph:	*The angel was right! I didn't tell you about it, because it seemed so impossible. But I dreamed that you were going to have a baby. Or at least I suppose it was a dream. Somebody in shining clothing told me, and whoever it was said that everything would be all right, that we should go ahead and get married.*
Mary:	O Joseph, the angel came to me, too, and told me that this baby will be called the Prince of Peace. His name will be Wonderful, Counsellor, the King of Kings. We are to name him Jesus. I'm scared, Joseph. Remember the prophecy, "And a virgin shall conceive, and her Son shall be called Immanuel, God with us." Do you think....
Joseph:	*I don't know, Mary. I do know that I love you, and that your child will be our child, and the rest we will leave to God.*
Mary:	Thank you, Joseph. Would you mind if I went to see Elizabeth, to tell her about this? I think she would understand, and I need to talk to someone.
Joseph:	*Go to Elizabeth — when you come back it will be time to travel to Bethlehem for the census. Do you think the baby will arrive before that?*

| Mary: | I'm afraid that the baby may be born in Bethlehem, Joseph. Now that's strange, isn't it? The prophecy says that the Messiah will be born of David's line. You're a descendant of David, aren't you? And Bethlehem is often called David's city. Maybe all of this has been planned. |

Narrator: In the meantime, God was busy making plans for another baby to be born. John, who would be known to the world as John the Baptist, would be born before Jesus. But listen, as Mary visits her cousin, Elizabeth.

| Elizabeth: | *Mary! Welcome! I am so glad to see you.* |

| Mary: | Peace to you also, Elizabeth. I bring strange news. |

| Elizabeth: | *No stranger that mine, Mary. Look at me! What do you see?* |

| Mary: | Why, you're pregnant! This is a miracle, Elizabeth. I'm so happy for you. |

| Elizabeth: | *Thank you, Mary. Not only is it a miracle, but the moment I saw you the baby moved within me. Surely your good news must be as wonderful as mine.* |

| Mary: | It is, Elizabeth. I'm having a baby too. I wanted to share my news with you, and coming here to do that has meant that I am able to share yours as well. I believe that God has blessed both of us. |

Elizabeth:	*I hope so, Mary. Another strange thing has hap-pened—Zachariah has been struck dumb. But yet he seems so happy about the baby, almost as though he knew about it before I did.*
Mary:	Your baby *will* be special, Elizabeth. And I know that Zachariah will speak again, and maybe someday we will all understand what God is doing in our lives. I believe that with all my heart.

Scripture
   Magnificat: Luke 1:46b-56
(Mary reads 46b-55, Narrator reads 56)

Narrator: Elizabeth had her son. She called him John, and Zachariah spoke again, and told of how an angel had visited him to tell him about the baby. He could hardly believe that such an old couple could have a child, so the angel struck him dumb until the baby arrived.

Mary returned to Joseph and they prepared for the trip to Bethlehem, to be counted in the census. You know the rest of the story—the Inn that had no room, the stable offered as a last resort, the shepherds and the angels, the star, and the birth. Let us sing together.

Hymn
   "O Little Town of Bethlehem" (#421 HB)

Mary:	My baby. Born in a stable. Hardly a proper birthplace for a King, my darling, but we could do no better. The stable is warm, the straw is soft, and you are loved.

I don't think I'm going to tell people about the angel that told me you were arriving, Jesus. They wouldn't understand. Whatever God has planned for you, it's obviously going to take some time to come to pass. You're just a baby, and your father and I will love you and care for you as our very own. I know that Joseph can hardly wait until you're old enough to go out to the workshop with him! But it's my breast that you're wanting now, and you and I will be closer than any other mother and child, because I know that you're very, very, special.

I mustn't be too proud of you, though. Every woman thinks her baby is special. Maybe there's a little bit of God in *every* baby. I wonder if that's something you'll be able to explain when you grow up? But I mustn't think of what is to come. For now you are my baby, and I love you. Sleep, baby Jesus, sleep.

Hymn
  "Rocking Carol" or "Away in a Manger" (#419 HB) ♪

CANDLE-LIGHTING

Leader: Any candles we light during worship have their source in Jesus Christ, the Light of the World. And so we light the central candle. (Light white candle.)

Candle-lighter: *The Word was the source of life, and this life brought light to humankind. The light shines in the darkness, and the darkness has never put it out.*

Leader: Other candles can be lit from the central candle to remind us of different things. In the Advent wreath the four candles usually symbolize joy, peace, hope and love. These two candles will be for us the mother and father of Jesus — Mary, the blue candle, and Joseph, the brown.

Candle-lighter: *The colour blue has always been associated with Mary. Blue for her purity, blue for the Queen of Heaven. Hail Mary, the angel said, blessed art thou among women, and blessed is the fruit of thy womb, Jesus.*

Leader: We have chosen for Joseph the colour brown.

Candle-lighter: *Joseph, descendant of David, do not be afraid to take Mary to be your wife. She will have a son, and you will name him Jesus.*

If you are using individual candles, continue as follows, otherwise announce closing hymn.

Leader: Come now, light your candles from the source of all light, and may our lights shine so brightly that all who see them may know that we worship the Christ, the Light of the World.

Light individual candles during singing of hymn and if there is a large group, worshipping within a sanctuary, have people stand around the outside aisles of the church holding their candles. Turn sanctuary lights down.

Hymn
   "Silent Night" (#416 HB) *3*

      Leader: These candles must be extinguished, but re-
                           member that the Light of the World shines on
                           and on, and the darkness will *never* put it out.
                           Go in peace.

Being the Light

If possible, have an arrangement of candles as your worship centrepiece. Use candles of different colours, different sizes, with one larger and taller than the others, to represent Jesus, the light of the world. There should be at least one candle for each person you expect, for use in the program section.

WORSHIP

Call to Worship
People whose vision is impaired, or who have been blind from birth, can often distinguish between darkness and light. We who have eyes that see can glorify God for the beauty of sunrise and sunset. All who know God can rejoice in the enlightenment we experience through God's son Jesus, the light of the world. Let us worship our God whose first task in creation was to say, "Let there be light." (Gen. 1:3) (Light central candle)

Prayer

God of illumination and majesty, we praise you for the gift of light, for the gift of sight. Open our eyes that we may see more than your world of beauty, more than the faces of our loved ones. Help us to see with the eyes of our hearts that we have been gifted with the good news of the gospel, and help us to spread the light of that gospel to all whom we meet. Amen.

Hymn

"Let There Be Light" (#274 HB)

Scripture

Luke 2:22-38

REFLECTION

There is a problem in talking about God as light, for not all can see light with their eyes. There is also a new awareness that when we categorize light as good and darkness as evil, those whose *skin* is dark may feel excluded from many of our liturgies, liturgies which exalt light and condemn darkness.

There is no possibility, however, of ignoring the implication of light in the Bible. From the beginning of creation, through Moses and the burning bush and all of the Psalms, in the nativity stories and the flames of Pentecost, light means revelation, illumination, the presence of God, and all that is good in life.

At the time of his Epiphany, Jesus was brought to the temple for the normal Jewish ritual that took place so many days after the birth of a child. It was a temple priestess, Anna, and an old man named Simeon, who were able to see the importance of this particular child. Anna had been praying and working and waiting for years for the appearance of this special person, someone who would be the Saviour of her people. We have no idea what brought about this recognition. Many babies were brought to the temple regularly — why did she notice Mary and Joseph and their newborn child?

Or do we need to ask that question? The importance of the Epiphany story is not that Anna and Simeon recognized Jesus as the Messiah, but that he *was* the Messiah. That fact would be proven again and again. This tiny child whom Anna blessed, this baby whose existence relieved the mind of Simeon so much that he was able to die a happy man, grew to become Jesus of Nazareth, Saviour and Redeemer of the whole world.

For us, the showing forth of Jesus reminds us that not only was Jesus the light of the world, but that he told his followers that they too were light. They were salt and yeast, challenged to permeate the hearts of people; they were told to let their light shine, not to hide it. It follows that *we* are salt and yeast, *we* are light. We have this obligation to tell the story, to show through our own lives what it means to be followers of the Christ. It is an awesome responsibility.

Prayer

Gifted, we seek to gift others. Aware, we desire that others share our awareness. Blessed, we try to be a blessing. Help us, O God, to keep the light of our faith burning brightly so that all who see and know us may see and know your Son Jesus, revealed in us as you were revealed in him. Amen.

PROGRAM

Ask members of the group to light one of the candles from the central candle. Suggest that as each person chooses a candle to light, they consider sharing any particular reason why they chose it — the colour, the size, or position, for instance. (Remember that only those lighting the first candles have any real choice.)

Take time to discuss the responses to the choosing of candles. It could be that someone might be able to share personal feelings, such as being in a "blue mood," feeling "fat and ugly," or "insignificant." This is an opportunity to stress that it is the *light* which is important, and to note that all of the candles give off the same amount of light, regardless of their size or beauty.

We acknowledge that Jesus is the light of the world. We find it more difficult to imagine that we are also called to let our light shine, since that implies that we may actually be on a par with Jesus. Discuss this. Conclude this discussion by quoting a poster which says, "There are two ways of being the light: to be the candle, or to be the mirror that reflects it."[5] Then discuss the difference between these two concepts. Are there people comfortable with one and not the other? Can we help people find the confidence to *be* a light, rather than a reflector? Should we?

Light is completely irrelevant unless there is something to illuminate. The familiar children's hymn says that, "Many kinds of darkness in the world are found ..."[6] Take some time now to list some of the dark things in this world that need the illumination of Christ's light. The list is almost endless.

Following this listing, ask members to select one area where they could "make their light shine" during the following week. It could be a visit to the darkness found in the home of a person with alcoholism or Alzheimer disease; a note or card to brighten the day of a shut-in; a letter to a politician regarding the dark shadows of violence in our cities and towns; or a time of prayer for those suffering the darkness of mental illness.

If your group is small, give each person a tiny birthday candle to take home as a reminder of their need to be a light.

Twelfth Night

WORSHIP

Call to Worship
A long time ago, astrologers made an important journey because of what they saw as they studied the stars. Many people follow their dreams, walking down an imaginary "yellow brick road" or "hitching their wagon to a star" to look for something that they cannot fully understand yet feel compelled to seek. In worship we acknowledge the same inner compulsion to seek the presence, the forgiveness, and the love of God, just as those who followed the star to the manger in Bethlehem so long ago.

Prayer
We don't understand what compels us to seek someone or something greater than ourselves, O God, but we are thankful for that desire which exists within us. You have made us so that our hearts are restless, until they find rest in you. You have made us yearn for you as an animal pants for water. Quench our thirst, calm our restless hearts with the awareness of your presence here and now. Amen.

Hymn
"I Am the Light of the World" (#24 SGP)

Scripture
Matthew 2:1-12

REFLECTION

It has been traditional to include the story of the Magi within our Christmas celebrations, but in actual fact this visit happened some years after the birth of Jesus. Two references support this: The visit was made to a house, rather than a stable, (Mt. 2:11) and the story of Herod causing all children under two years of age to be killed, so that this baby, sought by the astrologers, would die. (Mt. 2:16) Both references indicate more of a time lapse than normally understood. Celebrating the arrival of the Magi on January 6 recognizes this time difference.

Conversely, saving the visit of the Magi for January 6 seems to give them more importance and helps us emphasize the Epiphany, or showing forth of Jesus. Epiphany tells us that this baby, regardless of the date of his birth, was to become the saviour of the whole world. The visit of the wise men from the east broadens the base of interest. This is why Epiphany is an important time to consider how our church groups and congregations reach out to the whole world, how well we obey the great commission to go into all the world, teaching and preaching. (Mt. 28:19)

In recent years many Christians have come to believe that we are not the only ones to whom God has been revealed. This is very difficult for those of us who grew up thinking that once the whole world believed in Jesus, the Kingdom of God would be here. For many centuries Christians have sent out missionaries to "convert the heathen" and in that way help to bring in the Kingdom.

Now we understand that the so-called "heathen" have had valid revelations of the divine in their own religion. We have come to accept that people of other faiths have the right to believe that God has been revealed to them through Buddha, through Mohammed, or through creation, just as we believe that God is fully revealed in the life, death, and resurrection of Jesus.

The important fact of the Epiphany may be not that Jesus was revealed as God's son, but that God was made known. We therefore celebrate the fact that this one God has been revealed in countless ways, to many people, at different times. At the same time, we acknowledge that, for Christians, the revelation of God came to us through the person of Jesus who was recognized by foreigners, led to his home by a star.

Prayer
Keep our minds open, we pray, so that we can broaden our horizons. Keep our minds focused, we pray, so that we remain faithful to the inheritance we have received from generations of Christians who have proclaimed in faith, "Jesus is Lord." Give us strength and courage to declare that he is also the way, the truth, and the life. Amen.

PROGRAM

There are twelve days between Christmas and Epiphany. The twelve days of Christmas. January 6th is often called Old Christmas Day, and in some areas it is traditional to take down the Christmas decorations on this day. Another Twelfth Night tradition is a cake, with one bean baked in it. When the cake is shared the person who receives the piece with the bean in it is supposed to be favoured with a very good year ahead. (If you decide to make one for your refreshments it might be wise to use a cherry instead of a bean, to avoid any dental accidents.)

Bring up the subject of interfaith relationships very carefully. Remember that while some people are very open to the idea of "sharing heaven" with Jews, Muslims, and Buddhists, others are firm in their belief that Jesus Christ is the *only* way to God. We need the confidence that comes with assurance in order to be open to new possibilities.

Ask group members if any of them know people of another faith. If so, ask them if they could say something about their relationship with this other person or family. Do they share their religious beliefs? Have they invited their friends to some Christian celebrations and/or have they been present at festivals or celebrations of the other faith?

Some Christian denominations have stopped sending missionaries to foreign countries to convert people to Christianity. Instead they work with partner churches in developing countries, training leaders and teachers, and helping people learn how to help themselves and how to worship God in their own traditions. What does your group think about the role of missionary today?

Does Epiphany challenge us to reach out to people of different races, different cultures, and different faiths? Discuss ways of doing this in your own situation.

Suggested Reading

Faith in My Neighbour (Toronto: The United Church Publishing House, 1994) examines different religions in Canada. Each chapter is written by a person from a different faith community. The book makes good reading and provides ample evidence that there are more similarities than differences between people of faith.

Winter

Beating the Blues

WORSHIP

Call to Worship
"Why art thou cast down, O my soul? and why art thou disquieted in me? Hope thou in God: for I shall yet praise my Saviour and my God." (KJV Psalm 42:11) Those words are from Psalm 42 and they express the way many of us feel occasionally, and especially in January.

Hymn
"As Longs the Hart" (#89 SGP) or "Just as I Am" (#284 HB)

Prayer
Forgive us, O God, when our souls are disquieted — when we feel "blue." Give us the hope of the psalmist, so that we may turn sighs to hymns of praise, and times of despair to joyous living. In Jesus name, Amen.

Scripture
Ecclesiastes 3: 9-15

REFLECTION

There is no more depressing book in the Bible than Ecclesiastes. Unless it's Job, maybe. The whole theme of the Philosopher who wrote the book of Ecclesiastes is that "life is useless." Many people have wondered why the book was included in the Bible. In the introduction to the book found in the *Good News Bible* an attempt is made to answer that question. It claims that the book illustrates that biblical faith is broad enough to take such attitudes into account."...the same bible which reflects these (depressing) thoughts also offers the hope in God that gives life its greater meaning."[7]

In other words, it gives credibility to our feelings of depression — we are not the first to feel blue, nor will we be the last. And while the Philosopher's advice to those who feel that life is useless is to "eat, drink, and be merry," Psalm 42 expresses the hope that the one who is cast down *will yet* praise God.

That is our hope — that we will feel better soon — that tomorrow we will be able to praise God with joy. But modern psychologists tell us that sitting around hoping that our feelings of depression will go away is often not successful. Far better to make an effort to put something positive in the place of our negative feelings — go for a walk, call a friend, have a party. Most of us know what we need to do to pull ourselves out of our "blue funks," but we often have to make a very intentional effort to get started.

We also need to differentiate between the usual January blues and serious depression that requires medical help. It's often difficult for a casual acquaintance to tell the difference. Attempts to make a severely depressed person "cheer up" may have the opposite effect.

But our theme is *beating* the blues! And one time-honoured way to do that is to sing.

Hymn

"Come, Thou Fount of Every Blessing" (#52 SGP) or "Joyful, Joyful We Adore Thee" (#19 HB)

PROGRAM

See if you can read the following with a straight face, just for fun.

> A tong lime ago, a daggy shog was bossing a cridge over a pillmond, carrying a harge lunk of boast reef in his mipping drouth. He looked down and saw his own wace in the fawter, just like a remection in a flirror.
> Of course he thought it was aduther nawg, with a meece of peat bice as twig as his! So he mopped his own dreece of peat, and flitterally lew at his rewatron in the flecture. Naturally, he was aquazed to find that he not only mawst the leat he had, but that he narn dear liced his loff! Storal to this mory: If you want to hay stappy, never mance into a gleerer![8]

Spend five to ten minutes sharing the various techniques people have for cheering themselves up, for "beating the blues." If the group is large, divide into groups of five or six so that everyone can participate.

A common cause of mild depression can be a poor self image. Sometimes when we're "blue" we feel like singing the old song — "Nobody loves me, everybody hates me ..." But before anybody really wants to love us, we have to learn to love ourselves. Have your group do the following exercise:

1. Pair off, preferably with someone you don't know very well.

2. In five minutes of conversation, each person writes a list of all the things that the *other* person does well. Some people need a little persuasion to reveal their talents.

3. Exchange lists with your partner and read each of your abilities as an "I" statement (e.g. "I play the piano"). (It's important to keep this stage of the process under wraps while the earlier conversations are taking place, or people may be reluctant to share their talents.)

This may seem like we're "blowing our own horn" but what's wrong with that? We're loving and capable people, and we need to remember that.

After the exercise is over, invite people to complete the following statement about their partner: "The thing I admire most about you is ...." If the group is small these can be shared with the whole group. In a larger group they could simply be shared with the partner.

Finish the program by challenging everyone to do something nice for themselves during the coming week. You can bring the discussion full circle by reminding the group of the "cheer up" techniques they listed after the shaggy dog story.

Justice

WORSHIP

Call to Worship

"But let justice roll down like waters, and righteousness like an ever-flowing stream." (Amos 5:24) The words of the prophet Amos roll off our tongues as easily as the river water ripples over stones and rocks on its relentless way to the sea. Too often "justice" is translated as "just us," and we easily forget that God is always on the side of those who are treated unjustly, those who suffer, and the poorest of the poor. Let us in awe and humility worship God.

Prayer

God of justice, God of righteousness, forgive us when we do not act out in our lives the words we say we believe. Forgive us when we speak of rights without responsibilities; when we are proud of helping the poor when they seem deserving; and when we think the solution to the problems of our society involves changing the living standards of everyone except ourselves. Have mercy upon us, for the sake of your son, Jesus, in whose name we pray. Amen.

Hymn

"Thy Kingdom Come — On Bended Knee" (#278 HB)

Scripture

Numbers 27:1-11 (Don't worry about the correct pronunciation of the names in this passage — read it for the story it tells.)

REFLECTION

The Old Testament is full of interesting stories, but they are often hidden among words that we cannot pronounce. Names of people and places are unfamiliar to us, and we find it difficult to sift through the tedious parts to really get into the story. The five daughters of Zelophehad are good examples. Their father's name, their names, are strange to our ears, and the story sometimes makes us feel as though we were reading some dry legal document.

This is the story of five women who dared to stand before Moses, the great leader of their people. They had a problem and they thought that he should do something about it. We are beginning to place more emphasis on stories of women in the scriptures. These five are an excellent example of women seeking justice; standing up, quite literally, for their rights. When we delve a little deeper into the whole story we realize that the real significance may be the preservation of the *father's name*, not the inheritance of the daughters.

Without speculating about the underlying reasons for including this story in the writings selected for the canon, or Bible, we can admire these women, and use them as role models for our own actions. Today women are standing up for their own rights, and, more importantly, they are standing up for the rights of other women. Centuries of living in a patriarchal society has meant that women are often denied their basic rights. There are more poor women than poor men. Women are more often victims of violence. There are more single-parent families headed by women than those headed by men.

As we move into the 21st century we find that most women provide part, if not all of their family income as well as assuming the major responsibility for running the family home. And in their senior years, because they often outlive their partners, women often have to face their old age without financial security. These are familiar statements, which can be backed up with statistics. There are groups for women wanting to leave an abusive partner, or for those having problems as a single parent. These groups are often formed and staffed by women who have come through similar circumstances and who can offer realistic support.

The flip side of the coin is that many women who live in comfortable, stable relationships see no need to speak out for the rights of other women. We can learn from the five daughters of Zelophehad to stand up and speak out. We can find similar "gutsiness" in the woman who challenged Jesus, saying that "... even the dogs eat the crumbs that fall from their master's table." (Mt. 15:27) We find the tactic of persistence in the parable of the Widow and the Judge (Luke 18:1-8). Nevertheless, the example that Jesus set throughout his life clearly asks us to stand up and speak out and act for *others*, not just ourselves. "... truly I tell you, just as you did it to one of the least of these who are members of my family, you did it to me." (Mt. 25:40)

Prayer
Give us courage, O God, to speak out wherever we see injustice. If we suffer injustice in our own lives allow it to teach us to be understanding of others. Make us more supportive of our communities, because we know that justice cannot be a personal issue. Real justice requires cooperation, and people who are dedicated to working together for a just society. Help us to do our part, we pray. Amen.

PROGRAM

Give a brief synopsis of the scripture read during worship (Numbers 27:1-11) and then read the second part of the story of Zelophehad's daughters (Numbers 36:1-11). The discussion can be centred around the following questions:

Q Why do you think Moses, the priests, and the men in the community were willing to approach God so that the daughters were able to inherit their father's property?

A *It was important that a man's name be carried into the next generation. If the daughters did not inherit and maintain the property their father's name would be lost. This is why having sons was so important to the people of the Israelite tribes.*

Q What legal precedent was set by God's response?

A *The right of female children to inherit, although this is still not the case in many societies.*

Q Why was the concern about whom the daughters might marry so important to the male relatives?

A *If they married outside their tribe their husbands would inherit the property, and again, Zelophehad's name would disappear.*

Q What is the difference between the first decision (Numbers 27:8) and the second (Numbers 36:6)?

A *The first time Moses asked God to make the decision, the second time Moses made the decision himself. Also, the first decision was done in a religious context, while the second involved only the male heads of ancestral houses.*

Note verse 10 of the 36th Chapter: The daughters did as they were advised by Moses and their male relatives. Can you relate this to the way women sometimes act today?

Is there still a tendency for couples to desire a male child so that the father's name can be continued? What does this say to our female children?

To close, take a few moments for practice and then repeat together the beautiful words of the prophet Amos: "... let justice roll down like waters and righteousness like an ever-flowing stream."

Suggested Reading

The Women's Bible Commentary, edited by Carol A. Newsom and Sharon H. Ringe (Louisville, KY.: Westminster/John Knox Press, 1992)

Stewardship

WORSHIP

Call to Worship

We have been given so much, and yet we often find it difficult to look after all of our real or perceived needs. Sometimes we make unwise decisions regarding our finances, sometimes we fail to take responsibility for our God-given talents, or our God-given world. During our worship period, let us think of our responsibilities as managers of all we possess.

Prayer

Creator God, we know that your creation could provide the necessities of life for all of the world's people, if the resources of this planet were managed responsibly. We know that we ourselves could share more of our money and our time and our talents to support the work of our faith communities. Forgive us, we pray, for not responding to your call, for not sharing and giving as we know you want us to do. Help us to feel your presence with us now, and may all that we say and do bring honour and glory to your name. Amen.

Hymn

"God Whose Giving Knows No Ending" (#56 SGP) or "Take My Life and Let It Be" (#294 HB)

Scripture

Mark 12:41-44

REFLECTION

One definition of the word stewardship says that "Stewardship is what you do after you say, 'I believe.'" There are probably as many different definitions of "stewardship" as there are people within our churches whose ministry involves challenging people to share their resources of money, time, and talent.

Money is not the favourite topic of those who attend morning worship on Sunday mornings. Most people dislike being asked to increase their giving to the mission of the church, or to serve on yet another committee. But if all of us were to give with a real understanding of stewardship we would not need to appeal for funds. If we all gave one extra hour of our time to the mission of the church, through committees, teaching, visiting or outreach, the result would have a tremendous impact on the life and work of our congregations.

In some ways we act like advertising agencies — struggling to come up with new ideas to bring people to church and to get them to contribute their money and time to the church's programs. At the same time it seems that once they do become a part of our fellowship they are immediately drawn into our need to raise money, or recruit additional leadership.

Aren't we all missing the point, somehow? If we care enough to belong to an organization which seeks to proclaim God's will and purpose for the world, we must surely realize that this will require our financial support as well as our time and talent and energies. Think of the opportunities that we miss, because we are so busy raising money. Think of the possibilities that would expand before us if we all contributed some reasonable, and regular, proportion of our income. If all members were to give just four or five percent of their income to the church and its mission we would never need another financial campaign. Or a stewardship sermon, or program.

The story of the widow's mite is a familiar one. It reminds us of the importance of those who give little because they have little. Unfortunately, this story can be used to make a very small donation seem acceptable. We know in our hearts that it is the proportion of our giving that is important. The widow gave a small amount, but it was all she had. The boy who gave his small lunch to feed the multitudes is another example of such generosity. One hundred percent. Given because of all that was received.

Prayer
Eternal God, who gave us life and who gave your son to show us how much you love us, we know of no other way to respond to your love, except by giving in return. We offer all that we have and pray for the strength to manage it wisely. Amen.

Program

The international and ecumenical Fellowship of the Least Coin is based on the story of the widow's mite. Your group might enjoy learning a hymn written for this organization by Betty Turcott. It is called "Symbol of Hope"[9] and can be found in the Resources Section of this book.

Stewardship without guilt. Following the worship, you will need to lighten up a bit because of the strong feelings associated with money-talk. Try not to let people get defensive, and be sensitive to those in your group who may have very few financial assets.

Ask the group to suggest alternate ways of supporting the church, aside from their money and time. Recently we have been hearing about the stewardship of talents, trash, and tissue (organ donation) — three more T's to add to time and treasure. (There is a separate program in this book on the Environment, which deals with the way we could recycle, reduce or reuse our trash. You may wish to use parts of it with this one on stewardship.)

Have a talent search. Pair off members of your group and ask them to spend five minutes talking about some of the things they enjoy doing. Our talents are usually quite visible this way. Have each member of the pair report on the other person's talent, rather than having people share their own talents before the whole group. Talking about what we do well is difficult for many people, but with a little prompting we could come up with quite a list.

You might wish to follow this up by thinking of ways that each person's talents could be used, or combined, to enrich your group. This could involve raising money, or using some musical or dramatic talents to raise your spirits. Possibly someone with a particular skill, such as quilting or macramé, could get involved in teaching that skill to others.

The stewardship of tissue offers an opportunity to discuss organ and blood donor programs. There may be strong feelings around this issue. Allow people to share their feelings and talk about signing a donor card. If possible, acquire some information brochures from agencies involved with medical transplants before your discussion.

Alternate Program

Read, or have members read, the following scripture passages. After each one, ask the question, "What does this say about stewardship?"

Luke 17:5-6   If we had faith "as a mustard seed" could we concentrate on being the church and anticipate that members would want to support the work?

Luke 17:7-10   What does this say about people who want to give gifts to the church only if the donor's name is inscribed, or those who only contribute if they get something in return — like a meal, or a craft item selling at a tenth of its value?

Luke 8:1-3   Are the women in your church bearing too much of the fund-raising burden? Is this something to resent, or to be proud of?

Close your program with a challenge to all present to evaluate their givings of time, talent, treasure, trash and tissue.

Lent

The Lenten Journey

Worship

Call to Worship

As we journey through the Christian year, the time of Lent gives us an opportunity to reflect on how well we are following the way of Jesus, whom we call the Christ. We remember his desert times, his temptations, and we find confidence and strength to face the uncertainties of our own lives. Let us worship God.

Prayer

Gracious God, your son Jesus was lonely and tempted and yet willing to sacrifice his life for all humankind. We often feel incapable of walking in the path that he followed. Help us now, as we look again at one of the final acts of his earthly life. Accept our feeble attempts at discipleship through him, in whose name we pray. Amen.

Hymn

"Forty Days and Forty Nights" (#438 HB) or "There is a Green Hill Far Away" (#101 HB)

Poem - Morning Thoughts.
Season of Lent - leading up to Easter -

Scripture

John 13:12-17 -

REFLECTION

Lent has been traditionally a time of self-denial, of fasting and praying. It is also a time when we reflect on the last days of Jesus' life on earth. It is a time when we wonder if we are really deserving of the name "Christian." We wonder just how well we are doing in following the teachings of this man we call the Christ.

One of the most difficult of Jesus' teachings for us to follow is one we read about in John's gospel — the washing of feet. Many of us have allowed ourselves to almost "write off" this command of Jesus on the basis of the cultural and climatic conditions that no longer apply to modern society — especially modern North American society. We no longer wash people's feet when they arrive at our door, nor do we have servants to do this for our guests. This allows us to ignore the symbolism of the story, which is service to others.

Some faith communities have experimented with foot washing, or have substituted hand washing. A bowl of water and a towel placed on a table while the story is being read can also be quite moving. We do not need to re-enact the foot washing — we need to think about what such a servant attitude means to us. The visual aid helps us realize what that act must have meant to the disciples. Here was their master, acting as their servant. We who claim to have no worldly master or mistress, and who are unlikely to be able to afford servants, find it difficult to appreciate this role reversal of Jesus.

There is no doubt that Christians are called to *serve.* Lent is a time when we can evaluate our service, seek new ways to serve, or be strengthened to continue the service we are doing.

PROGRAM

Ask members to respond to the following questions, to make sure that everyone is aware of some of the traditions and meanings of the season of Lent.

Q Where does the word "Lent" come from?

A *From lengthening, as in the lengthening of days as spring approaches. The word "Lent" was often used interchangeably with "spring."*

Q How many days are there in Lent?

A *Forty, plus six Sundays.*

Q What is the significance of the number forty?

A *Forty days in the wilderness, forty years in the desert, probably just means "a long time."*

Q When does Lent begin and end?

A *The date of Easter was set by the Council of Nicea in 325 C.E. It is always the first Sunday after the first full moon of the spring equinox. Ash Wednesday, the beginning of Lent, is therefore 40 days and 6 Sundays before Easter Sunday.*

Q What is the liturgical colour of Lent?

A *Purple, signifying penitence and humility.*

After the questions, ask members to share their memories of Lent and its customs, and have them indicate whether or not they observe Lent in any particular way at this time of their lives.

Provide copies of the front pages and editorial pages of several recent newspapers. In pairs, ask members to scan the papers for stories of people acting and living in a Christ-like way. If your group is not too large, share these stories and any comments that arise from them.

Have one person take notes as members of the group list the various ways that Christians today express their faith in action during the Lenten season and also throughout the rest of the year. Encourage people to name the things they do themselves, as well as things done by others. Many acts of Christian service never make it to the front pages. Make an effort to comment on some of the ways people express their faith, affirming small actions as well as larger contributions.

Close by asking members to be intentional about their service during the following weeks.

Offering - Dedication

Hymn -

Closing

A LENTEN PRAYER

Lord Jesus Christ, by your passion, death and resurrection you have set us free from sin and death. May your grace renew our hearts this lent and help us turn from sin in our own lives. May we learn to appreciate more deeply the sacrifice you made for us. Accept our prayer, fasting and acts of charity as we seek to draw closer to you during this holy season. Strengthen the faith of your people so that we may be a sign of *your* love to all the world. Amen.

Acceptance

WORSHIP

Call to Worship

Everyone needs to belong, to feel loved, to be accepted. We join organizations, we form families, we behave in certain ways so that we experience these feelings. As we gather together in worship, let us make our acceptance of one another visible by joining hands.

Prayer

(If possible, lay this book aside and use your own words for the prayer, so the circle of acceptance is complete.) *Or:* Together we ask your blessing, O God, on the words of our mouths and the meditations of our hearts. Make your presence very real to us, make us aware of one another, as together we praise and glorify your holy name. We ask this in and through the name of Jesus, your Son, whose love, like yours, was unconditional. Amen.

Hymn

"In Loving Partnership" (#102 SGP)

Scripture
Luke 19:1-7

REFLECTION

There are many incidents in the gospels where Jesus is shown to be a person who accepts people as they are. He conversed with the Samaritan woman at the well, a woman rejected by her community and belonging to a culture which considered her almost untouchable. He spoke to the woman taken in adultery, telling her that he did not condemn her. Mary was just as much a friend of Jesus as Martha was; he accepted her listening just as he accepted Martha's hospitality. He noticed the little children who were being moved out of his way by the disciples, and compared them to the Kingdom of Heaven. He grieved when the rich man walked away from total commitment.

In the story of Zacchaeus we see Jesus reaching out again with sensitivity and acceptance. All Zacchaeus wanted to do was to find a spot where he could see Jesus. He didn't climb the tree to be noticed — he climbed it because he was short! And then, although Zacchaeus was certainly not a favourite with the crowd (tax collectors seldom are) he was asked to come down from the tree because Jesus wanted to stay at his house.

Naturally, those who felt closest to Jesus didn't like the idea very much. They wanted to have Jesus to themselves, they had important questions to ask him. They wanted to learn from him. And they were not able to accept Zacchaeus as Jesus did. They believed they were better than Zacchaeus, whom they saw as a rich tax collector, someone they called a "sinner."

It is so very easy to accept people who look like us, act like us, believe as we do. We have dozens of names for things that "belong" together — gaggles of geese, herds of cattle or sheep, schools of fish, flocks of birds, and congregations of people who share a similar faith. These things belong together. We teach our children to recognize things that belong together, so that when shown a picture of five animals and one flower, the child immediately sees that the flower "doesn't belong."

In God's creation, everything belongs. In spite of what humans have done to upset the balance of nature, we still marvel that large fish feed on smaller fish, weasels like chicken for supper, and plants that die in the winter live again in the spring to feed bees who need the nectar to make honey. Jesus spent his ministry teaching his followers that each and every person on this earth is important, each one of us is worthy of love and respect and acceptance. It hasn't been an easy lesson for us to learn. We are always ready to accept God's unconditional love, but reluctant to extend it to neighbours who are different or whose lifestyles we do not understand.

Prayer

We try to love our neighbour, God. In a general way. It's the specific situations which give us problems — people who abuse others, those who break laws and cause trouble, even those who irritate us or who ask us to change the way we do things. Help us to learn the lesson of acceptance, we pray, even when approval is difficult. Thank you for your unconditional love, and grant us the courage to reach out to others without being judgemental. Amen.

PROGRAM

Have group members name some real-life situations which make acceptance difficult. Responses will vary according to age, gender, community, and so on. In order to keep the group focused on the theme of acceptance, it may be necessary to keep challenging evidence of intolerance.

The following questions can help structure the discussion:

- Why is acceptance difficult for us?
- Is it possible that our intolerance is based on fear?
- What types of fears prevent us from accepting people as they are?
- How can Christians reflect Jesus' unconditional love in our own society?

As an alternative to asking the group for examples of intolerance, you may want to structure the discussion around recent examples of intolerance in your own community. Newspaper articles or a guest speaker can help stimulate discussion.

Close by assuring everyone that they are accepted and welcome in your group regardless of their responses during discussion. We do not have to agree with one another in order to accept one another.

Despair and Loneliness

WORSHIP

Call to Worship
The Psalms of the Hebrew Scriptures contain many cries for help. They often echo our own feelings and we wonder how it is that throughout history people have turned to God during times of despair. Psalm 130 begins, "Out of the depths I cry to you, O Lord. Lord, hear my voice! Let your ears be attentive to the voice of my supplications!" Let us worship the Lord, for we know that our cries for help are always heard.

Prayer
We are thankful that you hear our cries, O God. We are often overcome with feelings of doubt and despair, even though we may not have reached the "depths" of the Psalmist. We know that many people in our communities struggle daily with feelings of inadequacy, low self-esteem, and sometimes desperation. Sometimes we too despair and we turn to you so that our despair can change to hope. We believe that you want us to be present to people we meet, so that they may call on you through us. Help us to be open to the unspoken needs of those around us. Amen.

Hymn
"God When I Stand" (#125 SGP)

Scripture
Let us listen to another Psalm which cries out to God from the depths: Psalm 102:1-11

REFLECTION

This psalm is the prayer of a troubled young man, but many people have identified with its words. It is an extreme description of the way people feel when they are consumed by depression or loneliness. The first two verses form a cry for help; verses 3-11 describe the psalmist's situation: tormented, in pain, accused by enemies of being deserted by God. In those times, it was often believed that a person's problems were a sign that they were out of favour with God. The remaining verses of the Psalm, which we did not read, are words of praise to God, possibly a familiar hymn of the time.

Such an extreme description of loneliness serves two purposes: one, it makes our normal "down times" pale in comparison; and two, it helps us to understand that there are people whose suffering is very real, and very painful, because of their isolation or loneliness.

There are many whose loneliness involves a lack of friendly relationships and may therefore be eased through personal contact. People can gain a sense of belonging by joining a community group or church.

But there are many other reasons for depression and some are harder to mend — separation or divorce, being an isolated parent, trouble with the law, alcoholism, unemployment, chronic illness, shyness, or poverty. There is a need for us to minister to those who are on the margins of our communities, for any number of reasons.

No community of faith can solve all of these personal problems, but members can still learn to understand when to offer support and when to suggest expert help. We can reach out the hand of friendship and comfort, seek to simply "be with" people in their loneliness. To do so is to minister to them.

Prayer

We pray for all who are lonely, O God. Help us to reach out to those who are on the edges of our lives. We know that we cannot draw everyone into some cosy circle of love, but we can welcome those who do want to join us, and accept those who choose to remain outside. In our own times of personal loneliness enable us to reach out to one another rather than allowing our loneliness to fester. In the name of the one whose whole ministry was spent reaching out to others, Jesus our Saviour. Amen.

PROGRAM

Discuss openly the difference between reaching out to help someone and interfering in someone's personal life. Are we sometimes unwilling to risk the former because we are afraid of being accused of the latter?

Share some guidelines for identifying serious depression:

- a feeling that nothing can help
- no lightening of the mood, no indication of hopefulness
- a lack of self-esteem
- no desire to be with friends
- loss of appetite or excessive eating
- inability to sleep or constant need for sleep

Someone has suggested that we often reach out to people and yet feel that we have not helped that person. It is like reaching out to someone standing on the other side of a great chasm — our reaching out is not able to actually touch the person we are trying to help. If, however, we can put ourselves on the other side of the chasm, if we can actually *stand beside* the other person, our presence may be all the help that is required.

Ask members to suggest ways of standing beside people in the following situations:

- someone has been refused access to an apartment because of their race or because the landlord does not approve of their lifestyle
- someone is upset because the worship committee has suggested that the congregation stand for the reading of the gospel
- someone has just heard that their spouse has a malignant tumour
- someone has been the victim of spousal violence

You may wish to use some or all of these illustrations, or you may make up your own fictional situations which are more relevant for your group.

Be careful to end this program on a positive note. You could suggest that all members make at least one phone call during the week to someone who hasn't been active recently. Donating some personal care items to a transition house, a half-way house, or a mental health program in your area would also be a way of reaching out to people who are often lonely.

Easter

Easter

An Easter worship centre would make this meeting a little special: flowers, an Easter banner, or just a few ordinary eggs in a basket.

WORSHIP

Call to Worship

"I am the resurrection and the life," said Jesus, "Those who believe in me, even though they die, will live." (John 11:25)

Prayer

Dear God, your son Jesus also said that those who believed without seeing were indeed blessed. We did not see the wounds on Christ's feet, or the mark of the sword in his side, but we believe that because of his life, death, and resurrection we too shall inherit eternal life. Accept our doubts, O God, keep our faith strong, and be with us in our lives today as well as in eternity, through the presence of your Holy Spirit. Amen.

Scripture
Luke 24:1-11

Hymn
Choose your favourite Easter hymn

Reflection

Women were the first to know about the resurrection. That fact has been celebrated in recent years, as the church begins to take note of the role of women in the Bible, and as women seek to find new meaning for scripture in their own lives.

Many women have shared an experience that can help us understand the idea of resurrection, of life after death. That experience is childbirth. Modern medicine assures us that what happens to a child before it is born is crucial to that child's future development. If a pregnant woman uses drugs, she endangers her child. On the other hand, some women read stories to their unborn baby, or sing songs and play classical music, hoping that this will influence the child within their womb.

In other words, the nine months before birth are preparing the human being for its next "three score years and ten" — the Biblical calculation of a lifetime. (A "score" is twenty years.) Today, that probably should read four score years, and for some strong healthy people, even five.

Is it possible, then, that our years — seventy, eighty, or a hundred of them — are preparing us for our *next* life? We assume that the unborn child does not spend nine months wondering what comes next, why then should we worry about *our* next life?

Being born cannot be an easy process for the child, and dying is seldom easy either. But if we die and erupt into another life, a life as different from this one as the watery womb is different from the outside air, surely that is something to celebrate, not to dread. Loving arms of parents await the newborn and we are confident that God's love and care awaits us. How then, can we be afraid?

Prayer

You have made us, O God, so that we always have a desire to understand that which seems a mystery to us. Thank you for making us like this. Thank you for holding the details of our next life from us, just as we assume the details of this world are a mystery to the unborn. We trust you. We know you love us and understand our searching. Amen.

PROGRAM

To stimulate discussion around the scripture passage which was read, ask group members if they can identify any "stones" that are in the way of women's full participation in the life of your faith community. Does "tradition" block women from taking certain offices or positions? Is the stereotype of serving coffee and looking after children preventing some women from serving on finance committees, for instance?

Identify as many obstacles (stones) as you can, and then work at ways of "rolling away" any barriers that keep women from full and active participation. Are there ways to encourage women to be more active participants? (Training events, for example, or a workshop on parliamentary procedures?)

Questions which might encourage discussion:

- What do women do in our congregation?
- What do men do in our congregation?
- Who has power?
- Who is listened to?
- Are there areas where women might participate more fully in our congregation?
- Are there areas where men might participate more fully in our congregation?

To close, challenge your group to choose and implement one of their suggestions for encouraging more active participation.

Alternate Program
Give members of the group an opportunity to comment on ideas about life and death and life after death. Sharing beliefs and feelings about resurrection may consume all the time you have available for your program. Be sure to allow for differences of opinion — this is definitely a topic where no one has all the answers.

Crocus Minded

The book *Bless This Mess & Other Prayers* by Jo Carr and Imogene Sorley (1969) used the expression "Crocus minded"[10] to describe the condition of being willing to speak up, to risk, to stick out one's neck. The phrase has now become accepted as descriptive of people who do such things, especially those who do them out of the convictions of their faith. Crocus minded people are also called Easter people.

WORSHIP

Call to Worship
"It takes *courage* to be crocus minded ..."[11] and it takes another type of courage to bring our offerings of praise and adoration to our God. Let us bravely approach God, knowing the weakness of our faith, knowing also the richness and strength of God's love.

Prayer
God of the crocus and daffodil, God of victory and resurrection, we come with joy and thanksgiving, praising you for the glory of

spring, for the miracle of resurrection. Forgive us when we want to wait for a more opportune time to do your will, and help us to struggle against the human desire to procrastinate. Your word teaches that *now* is the time to act, *now* is the time to love, and we pray for the courage to do so. Amen.

Hymn
"Rise Up, O Saints of God" (#47 SGP)

Scripture
Mark 5:25-34

REFLECTION

The woman who dared to touch the hem of Jesus' garment was definitely crocus minded! She approached Jesus as an unclean woman, a very daring act. This woman had been suffering for twelve years with severe bleeding. While women today may be able to imagine the distress of such a physical problem, it is almost impossible for us to imagine what such a condition meant to a woman living in those days. She was probably a wealthy woman, since she had money to spend on doctors, but her constant hemorrhaging meant that she was continually ritually unclean.

That meant that anyone she touched became unclean, any piece of furniture her body touched became unclean. Males so affected by her touch would then have to engage in various cleansing rituals — a nuisance they would try to avoid by ignoring her. Since she was not allowed to take part in community activities while bleeding, she may have been ostracized by women as well. Maybe it was complete desperation that made her decide to seek out Jesus in the crowd, to realize that if she could just touch his clothing she could be restored to health.

Or it could be that, having tried everything else, she was not about to let this opportunity pass by, no matter how much of a long shot it was. That's called hope. Having faced much hard ground in her struggles, she was willing to push some more, to move some stones if need be, to be able to bloom in the light, rather than be forced by her disease to live in the shadows. The woman was healed, and because of that healing she was restored to her rightful place in the community. All because she was willing to reach out to connect with the power she sensed in Jesus.

It is not only serious illness that prods us into making a connection to something greater than ourselves, to seek some source of power and confidence. Sometimes we are reluctant to push ourselves into positive action to solve more ordinary problems. Maybe we've always wanted to learn another language, but feel that we're too old. Maybe we've been itching to get our hands on a computer, but have been afraid to venture into this new territory. Or maybe we have grown disillusioned with our church and now need to reach out in faith to a renewed relationship with Jesus. Do we need to touch the hem of his garment?

Prayer

We each have our own reasons for not pushing up into the light of a demanding faith, O God. We find it comfortable to stay protected, even isolated. We need your assurance that there is light and help available, that this is a beautiful world and that we have a role to play in it. Make us crocus minded, we pray, for there are things that we need to do, for ourselves, and for you. Amen.

PROGRAM

We admire, and possibly envy, those who struggle against incredible odds to make their mark upon society:

- A woman who uses a wheelchair works tirelessly (but not without tiredness) as a city councillor.
- A person with multiple sclerosis spends hours of her time and precious energy raising money to research a cure for the disease.
- A single mother completes her education and finds work to support her children.

Ask group members to briefly tell some stories of people they have known who have pushed themselves for a worthwhile cause. Do such stories ever cause feelings of guilt? Why?

Ask members to spend some time in silence as they think about the following questions. The answers do not need to be shared with the group unless someone offers to do so.

- Is there something I would like to do but am unwilling to take the risk?
- Is there someone who might be willing to rise to a challenge if I were to encourage him or her?

Can a *group* be crocus minded? If your group wanted to stick its neck out what might be a worthy cause to champion? (Family violence, congregational renewal, or alcohol and drug abuse, for instance.) Select one topic and list some appropriate actions. Then do a "pro and con" scenario. If the group decides to proceed, wonderful. If it decides to take no action at this time the exercise is still worthwhile. There will be other opportunities, other challenges.

In closing, suggest that members watch next week's news intentionally, to note stories of people who are "crocus minded," people who are speaking out against injustice or taking positions that involve personal risk.

Joy

WORSHIP

Call to Worship
It may be helpful to restrain our alleluias during Lent, but there is no need to confine them to Easter Sunday. Every day has its own alleluia kind of joy for those who believe that *nothing* can separate us from God's love, because of the life, death, and resurrection of Jesus Christ. Let us begin our worship with an alleluia!

Hymn
"Alleluia, Alleluia, Give Thanks" (#34 SGP) or your favourite hymn of joy

Prayer
We feel joyful as we offer you our alleluias, O God. We praise you for the gift of your Son, and for his wish that we might have abundant life. Forgive us if sometimes we lose sight of the joy that should be ours. Forgive us for finding it easier to complain than to compliment, to wish for things rather than rejoicing in what we have and sharing it. Let your joy and peace enter into our lives, we pray, in Jesus name. Amen.

Scripture
Matthew 28:1-10

REFLECTION

This story is so familiar to us that we find it difficult to imagine how the two Marys felt when they discovered the empty tomb. The guards were, in today's idiom, "scared to death." The women were also filled with fear. But there was something else. Scripture says that they "left the tomb quickly with fear *and great joy*, and ran to tell the disciples."

Fear and joy seem to be an unusual combination. Yet anyone who fearfully awaits a medical test result and then hears the words, "It's OK, the lump is just a cyst" knows that there is a definite connection between the depths of our fear and the height of our joy. In what is probably a more difficult situation, many families have gone from the joy of a teenager's graduation to the fear standing around a hospital bed, following a motor vehicle accident. Fear and joy may not exist together, but they do sometimes follow each other around.

In the scriptures the word "joy" is often used to describe the feelings which follow forgiveness, reconciliation, or some kind of trouble, such as war or famine. If we look at the things which bring us joy — our families or our hobbies, for instance — we can easily see that accident or separation within our families or the loss of treasured photographs, can easily turn joy into sorrow.

In the same way, when an adult child comes to visit after a long absence the sadness of missing him or her becomes instant joy. The frustration of a potter, seeking the perfect shape, becomes a joyful thrill of accomplishment once the piece is finished.

A certain minister's wife started a J-Joy group in many of the churches her husband served. She sought out older women, gathered them together, showered them with cheerful poems and stories, and shared with them her own joyful philosophy of life. Her joy is the contagious kind. The name of the group was an acronym — J for Joy, which follows when Jesus is first in our lives (J), others come next (O), and you think of yourself last (Y).

We cannot all lay claim to the vivaciousness and charm that make people feel joyful simply by being around us. Some people just seem to be born that way. But we can all smile, we can all find something nice to say if we really try. We can remember the words of Jesus, found in John 15, verse 11, following his description of the relationship of the vine and the branches: "I have said these things to you so that my joy may be in you, and that your joy may be complete."

Prayer

We desire that complete joy, O God, that your son Jesus wished for us. The joy that you wish for all of your children. We know that there are sad things in this world, but prevent us from allowing sorrow and despair to defeat our capacity for joy. With the psalmist let us proclaim, "happy are the people whose God is the Lord." (Psalm 144:15b)

PROGRAM

Because joy and sadness are so interrelated, you will need to make a real effort to keep the group aware of the topic — which is *joy*, not sadness.

According to *Cruden's Concordance* there are three references to "sad" in the New Testament. In the *New Revised Standard Version*, however, in the story of the rich man, (Mk. 10:22) the word "sad" has been changed to "went away grieving." Again, when Jesus spoke of the proper way to fast in Matthew 6:16, the word "sad" is translated as "dismal" in the *New Revised Standard Version*. Only in Luke 24:13 does the word "sad" remain, describing the emotions of the two people who met Jesus, walking to Emmaus.

Have these passages read, and lead the discussion along the following lines:

Mark 10:17-27 The rich person in this story was unable to give up everything he owned to follow Jesus. If this made him go away sad, or grieving, what was it that gave him joy in life? Is there anything wrong with finding joy and happiness in possessions? Do you think this young man could have found even more joy in giving up his riches? Do you know of anyone who has done so?

Matthew 6:16 Most of us no longer "fast" as a way of showing our devotion to God. Substitute the word "worship" and discuss what this might say to us about our attitude on Sunday mornings. Who would be the "hypocrites" in this case and what would they be doing?

Luke 24:13-35 Death brings sadness. We do not need to wonder why these two people were sad. We do, however, need to finish the story to see them with burning hearts — surely a most profound type of joy. How is Jesus made known to those who follow him today? Does the breaking of bread (communion) leave us feeling as joyful as those in this story? If not, why not?

Here's a thought to ponder in closing: Should we expect to *find* joy when we come to worship or to a group meeting, or should we *bring* joy to both?

Suggested Reading

For an excellent reading on this subject see the chapter entitled "Joy and Sadness" in *The Prophet*, by Kahlil Gibran.

Pentecost

Pentecost

WORSHIP

Call to Worship
Pentecost is a birthday celebration! The birthday of the holy catholic church. Light the candles, blow up the balloons, open the windows of your hearts so that the wonderful winds of the Holy Spirit can enter. Let us praise God.

Hymn
"Spirit Divine, Attend Our Prayers" (#60 HB)

Prayer
Come to us as light, wind and fire, O God, as your Spirit came to those who gathered themselves together after Jesus' death and resurrection. Lighten our burdens, blow away our feelings of inadequacy and make our hearts burn within us. Empower us, we pray, to be instruments of your peace in our world. Amen.

Scripture
Acts 2:1-8,12-14

REFLECTION

This is one of the most exciting stories in the Bible. This is the birth of the Christian church, the church which has endured for twenty centuries. Pentecost has received more attention in recent years, due to the increased use of the Common Lectionary and a renewed emphasis on the various seasons of the church year. Congregations celebrate with balloons and banners and red candles, with a birthday cake for the children. Since red is the liturgical colour of Pentecost, some congregations ask people to wear something red to church on the day of Pentecost.

In the Jewish tradition Pentecost was the name given to the Festival or Feast of Weeks. It was a harvest festival, held fifty days after the beginning of harvest, which coincided with the Feast of Unleavened Bread, or Passover. The name "Pentecost" comes from the Greek word for fifty.

It is difficult for us to put ourselves in the place of those assembled on that Pentecost Day recorded in the book of Acts. Here, together in one place, were the disciples, who had finally accepted Christ's death and rejoiced in his resurrection. They had witnessed his ascension into heaven. They began "devoting themselves constantly to prayer, together with certain women, including Mary the mother of Jesus, as well as his (Jesus') brothers." (Acts 1:14) They had attended to the management details of their group life, replacing Judas who had hanged himself. Life went on, and they gathered together on the Day of Pentecost, according to their tradition.

But this was one Pentecost Day they would never forget. Wind, tongues of fire, and the ability to understand and speak other languages made the followers of Jesus appear drunk. But Peter recognized what was happening. He remembered his history, and claimed that this experience was nothing less than God pouring out God's spirit, as spoken through the prophet Joel, chapter 2, verse 28: "... I will pour out my spirit on all flesh; your sons and your daughters shall prophesy, your old men shall dream dreams, and your young men shall see visions."

The day ended with about three thousand persons being welcomed into what was to become the Christian church. And that same Spirit is available to us, is present with us, and is the source of our power and strength.

Prayer

God of fire and wind and light, make us aware again of the power of your Spirit. Strengthen us, make us bold. We pray especially, O God, that your Spirit will find its way into the hearts of all those who see violence as a way of life so that the young and old may see visions and dream dreams of peace. Amen.

PROGRAM

Celebrate Pentecost! Light red candles, tie red, orange, and yellow streamers on a small fan to symbolize the flames of the spirit, or make a banner.

To begin, ask how many present still live in the place where they were born, and attend the same church. Probably not many. Allow a few minutes for people to describe churches of their childhood, or churches where they first felt called to be an active church member.

If possible, give a brief history of the church to which you now all belong.

Following are some verses selected from the book of Acts, which indicate the presence of women in the early church. Write each reference on a slip of paper and ask different people to read them aloud, allowing time for discussion.

- Acts 6:1
- Acts 9:36-42
- Acts 12:11-12
- Acts 16:14-19
- Acts 17:4
- Acts 18:2-3, 18, 24-26

Obviously there were many women involved in the early church, often in positions of leadership. Why do you think that their stories are not generally as well known as stories of some male followers of Jesus?

At the first Pentecost all those present were able to understand what the people who were filled with the Spirit were saying. Today, some people try to use inclusive language so that others will understand them and be able to hear their message. For example, "human" or "person" refers to people in general instead of the masculine terms "mankind" and "man."

The way we use words defines our attitudes. If we speak about "firemen" instead of "fire fighters" it *implies* that only men can fight fires. If we continually refer to God with masculine pronouns we must believe that God is a man. Saying that God is a spirit while we use male pronouns to describe God is a contradiction.

As disciples, do we have a responsibility to try to keep up with the changes that have taken place in language? Should we make an effort to use language which will help people feel included and avoid terms that exclude?

Close with some illustrations of the changes that have taken place in our language. See if your group can give the inclusive terms for the following:

- policeman (police officer)
- fisherman (fisher)
- chairman (chair)
- man of letters (writer)
- manpower (labour)

Religious terminology can be a little trickier. See if your group can come up with some gender-neutral or female-oriented terms for worship. The idea is not to discard the familiar terms — like "God the Father" or "Prince of Peace" — but to enrich our spirituality by broadening the way we think.

Christ's Body, the Church

WORSHIP

Call to Worship
"And I tell you, you are Peter, and on this rock I will build my church and the gates of Hades will not prevail against it." (Mt. 16:18)

Hymn
"The Church's One Foundation" (#146 HB)

Scripture
At the end of the gospel of Matthew, after the account of the resurrection, Jesus asks the women to tell the other disciples to go to Galilee and he will meet them there: Matthew 28:11-20.

Prayer
Dear God, we pray for strength of spirit to be your church. Baptize us with your love that we may do your work. Guide us that we may teach by example the meaning of your word. Amen.

REFLECTION

The closing words of the gospel of Matthew have been considered as Jesus' commission to the church — go, baptize, teach — and his assuring words "... remember, I am with you always, to the end of the age" (Mt. 28:20b) have been a comfort to millions of Christians. Many of us know those words by heart.

The *New Revised Standard Version* of the Bible translates the great commission in this way: "Go therefore and make disciples of all nations, baptizing them in the name of the Father and of the Son and of the Holy Spirit, and teaching them to obey everything that I have commanded you." (Mt. 28:19-20a)

In the early church, believers were received into the church by adult baptism. The sacrament itself was preceded by training and teaching. The instruction to "make disciples" includes both baptism and teaching or apprenticeship. Since baptism was a one-time act the words seem to emphasize the teaching ministry of the new church. We still train and prepare men and women in this teaching function when they become set apart as ordained or commissioned ministers. Diaconal ministers (commissioned ministers in some denominations) stress the importance of education and service, and separate it from the ministry of word and sacrament.

Yet few people today consider teaching the most important function of a church. When it comes to calling a minister, most congregations say that the ability to preach good sermons is crucial. Those who value the place of music in worship feel that a fine music program is essential. Some say the most important thing about a church is the building itself, and suggest that serving the church means keeping the building in excellent condition. Of course, the Sunday School teachers would agree that teaching is primary in today's world, where little Christian education is given at home.

The church is teaching, preaching, music, and much, much more. If we take seriously the words of Jesus to "obey everything that I have commanded you" (Mt. 28:20a) we will love our neighbour as ourselves, look after the sick, care for the thief, the leper, the prostitute, and turn the world upside down! All of these things are possible only if the church is considered to be a "community" or "family" — a group of people working together, caring about one another, and caring about those in need outside of their community.

The church community comes together in worship so that men, women, and children can be prepared to go out into the world to help make the world a better place for all of its people and creatures. And that's a big order, isn't it? Which is why we have to keep coming back, and keep going out.

Prayer
Most gracious God, we humbly beseech thee for thy holy Catholic Church. Fill it with all truth; in all truth with all peace. Where it is corrupt, purify it; where it is in error, direct it; where any thing is amiss, reform it; where it is right, strengthen and confirm it; where it is in want, furnish it; where it is divided and rent asunder, make it whole again; through Jesus Christ our Lord. Amen.[12]

PROGRAM

In small groups, or together if your group is not a large one, use your imagination to create a "perfect" church. Use your own congregation as a start. What changes would be needed to make it qualify as "perfect"? Would you have a world famous preacher or would most of the preaching be done by lay persons? Would children be sent off to Sunday School for most of your service or would they be part of the church family? Would you improve your facilities? If so, where would the money come from? How about extra staff? You will need someone to record suggestions, so that you can have a picture of a "perfect" church in writing.

After this exercise see if there is *one* change that your group could initiate. Maybe it's as simple as having fresh flowers in church every Sunday, or as complicated as a Stewardship Visitation program to discover new sources of leadership and income. Why not do something about it?

Many denominations have declared themselves in favour of more involvement of children in all aspects of church life — taking part in worship, serving on committees, being involved in pastoral care and justice issues, as well as having an expanded share in the Christian Education program. This would certainly make some real changes in most of our congregations. How does your group feel about this?

Here are some discussion starters from a report of the United Church of Canada, entitled "A Place For You,"[13] from the section on "Justice":

- What are some of the ways in which children are treated unfairly by the "institutional" church?
- In what ways might your congregation be open to children's sharing of time, talent and treasures? List your ideas, and your suggestions for how to proceed on some or all of them.
- What concerns for the world have you heard children mention? List them, and reflect on your concerns for the world from your childhood.
- Suggest two ways children could be included in the planning and leadership of your congregation's outreach, justice or mission work.

- Children can handle knowledge of justice issues. Children should be spared knowledge of some justice issues. Which is right?
- Children seem to know intuitively what is fair and what is not fair. How is this intuitive knowledge like Jesus' perception of his world? How could this intuitive knowledge of children be part of a congregation's ministry?

Close by singing "I Am the Church, You Are the Church, We Are the Church Together."[14]

The Holy Spirit

WORSHIP

Call to Worship
We worship one God, but we believe that our God is revealed to us through Jesus Christ, and present with us in spirit, the spirit we call holy. Open your hearts and minds to the presence of that spirit as we seek the comfort, guidance and encouragement it offers. Let us worship in spirit, and in truth.

Prayer
Almighty and eternal God, you are spirit, you are Jesus, you are the source of the life we live. Your spirit is everywhere, as close to us as the air we breath, nearer than our hands and feet. Make us aware of your presence in this place, at this time, we pray, so that we may be enriched, strengthened and renewed. Amen.

Hymn
"Breathe On Me, Breath of God" (#240 HB)

Scripture
John 14:15-31

REFLECTION

The gospel of John is full of comforting words, but it also contains ideas that are difficult to understand. If we want to emphasize that God is neither male nor female, the constant reference to God as Father in this particular passage tempts us to avoid using it. We find it easy to pick out phrases like, "...peace I leave with you ..." (John 14:27a) or "...do not let your hearts be troubled ..." (John 14:27b) and ignore things like "On that day you will know that I am in my Father, and you in me, and I in you." (John 14:20) Most of us have some concept of the Trinity, made up of God, Jesus, and the Holy Spirit, but this passage implies that the disciples are part of that Trinity. We are in God; God, Jesus, and the Holy Spirit are all in us.

To add to our confusion, as children some of us were taught that the Holy Spirit is like our conscience. That fits in with the idea that the Spirit is within us, but it does have a negative effect. Our conscience reminds us of things which we shouldn't do, or makes us feel bad when we've done something wrong, rather than acting as the helper and advocate that Jesus promised. The old term "Holy Ghost" is another less-than-helpful description of the spirit. As children we learned to fear ghosts, not to look to them for comfort or support.

It is in the book of Acts that we find some sense of the *power* of the Holy Spirit. At Pentecost, when the promised Advocate or Helper did arrive there was wind and fire and the mystery of instant translation of everyone's language. The disciples became different people. They had received power, they preached and taught with renewed enthusiasm. They brought new people into their faith community, they began a movement which affected the rest of history.

For us, today, the Spirit can be many things. Our conscience which not only chides us when we make mistakes, but prods us to go forward in faith. A comforter who can surround us with the assurance of God's love, as a mother cuddles a child against her breast. And a source of power, especially when we seek that Spirit power in community. The Spirit is the source of power which can challenge and renew, power to effect change or to block change. The power that is already there, has been there since Pentecost, the power that is useless until it is "turned on."

Prayer

Turn *us* on, O God. Help us to reach out for the spirit power that your Son Jesus promised to those who follow his way. We seek this power, yet we need the Spirit in others ways as well. We need a comforter, a teacher, an enabler, so that the power is used wisely and well, to lead us into your eternal ways of truth. In Jesus name we pray, Amen.

PROGRAM

Assemble an assortment of "gadgets" in an opaque bag: kitchen tools, sewing notions, hardware — almost anything will do. Pass the bag around and have group members take one item from it, sight unseen. Once everyone has something from the bag, ask them to think about a possible connection between the "gadget" and the Holy Spirit. A tape measure, for instance, can indicate the way the Spirit helps people to "measure up." Something soft can remind us of the Spirit as comforter. A kitchen utensil might help us "turn over" a new leaf. Let people come up with their own ideas and have fun!

Someone coined the word "spirit-incidence." The word, like "providence," is used to describe circumstances which seem to be more than mere coincidence: Someone telephones moments after you have expressed your concern for them or a job loss leads to a new, more suitable type of work. Have your group members share some of the times when events have happened in their lives that they believe gave evidence of the Spirit in action.

Evangelical Christians feel very comfortable with the presence of the Holy Spirit in their midst. People in the reformed tradition are less apt to rise in church and give an extemporaneous prayer as a result of the "moving" of the Spirit in their heart. There are often extremes — one sometimes doubts the reality of the Spirit when testimonies and prayers become repetitive and prolonged, and yet one often wishes that the Spirit would put a smile on some churchgoer's faces, and a little more joy in their singing. Talk with your group about how your faith community experiences the Spirit.

Return to the mystery of the Trinity and the incarnation and discuss the implications of the disciples being part of the godhead. Does this mean that we, as modern disciples, have something of the divine in us? If so, does this say anything to us about the way we treat our bodies, the temple of the Spirit? Does it imply that when people are watching us go about our daily lives, they are watching God at work in the world? Can we learn to see the face of Jesus as we try to love the unlovely people in our lives?

Close by quietly singing together the first verse of the hymn, "Spirit of the Living God" (#91 SGP).

Summer

Affirmation

WORSHIP

Call to Worship

Jesus wanted to gather Jerusalem under his wings, as a hen gathers her chicks. We are told that we are held in the palm of God's hand. God's affirmation of each one of us was made visible in the birth, life, death and resurrection of Jesus, the Christ. Perhaps the most positive affirmation that we receive from the Bible is the well-known, well-loved, 23rd Psalm:

Scripture

Psalm 23 (Maybe someone could recite this from memory or sing #131 from the Hymn Book)

Prayer

Loving God, you have made us so that we need to be loved. Sometimes just knowing that *you* love us and care for us is not enough. We need human arms to hug us, human smiles to cheer us, and human words to make us feel good. Let us see this as strength, rather than weakness, so that we can reach out to others with the kind of love we need so desperately ourselves. Grant us your grace and your peace, Amen.

Hymn
"I Will Never Forget You, My People" (#71 SGP)

REFLECTION

There are posters around these days that say "I think I need a hug." It isn't easy for us to come right out and say those words. Often we think that those who love us should *know* when we need a hug or a phone call or a friendly note. We are reluctant to admit that we need "affirmation." Affirmation is one of those overused words that crop up every now and then, but whether we call it "fishing for compliments" or "seeking affirmation," we know that we mean this craving for approval, for love.

For many years now, women have been recovering and affirming the contributions of the thousands of women working in our churches and communities. This is more than the pat on the back, or the appreciation that we all crave. This is asking our churches to intentionally recognize that women are important, that women work hard and that they have made valuable contributions in church and community. In other words, women wish to be taken seriously.

Affirmation works. St. Paul knew about affirmation when he wrote to the different churches. Paul usually started his letters with warm words of encouragement, he listed the good things that the people had done, he told them that they were continually in his prayers. Only then did he get to their problems and his instructions for the proper way to live the Christian life.

Praise works wonders for children, and is often more effective than various forms of discipline. Praise can also be useful in the marketplace. There are companies who earn good money by telling bosses that they will get more work from their employees if they praise them as often as possible. There are studies that claim there can be an increase in production figures when praise is combined with other incentives. Not that women need their work affirmed so that they can do *more*, but this simply illustrates that affirmation is a recognized method of keeping a business, or a women's group, or a church, working well.

Prayer

Strengthened and affirmed by you, O God, we can go into the world with eagerness and joy to change things, to make a difference. That same strength allows us to affirm the lives and work of others, who are working in their own way to bring in the just society that is our common goal. Amen.

PROGRAM

Give each person in your group a small cotton ball. Call them "happy spots" and have members put small pieces of cotton on someone's shoulder as they pay them a compliment. One cotton ball can make many "happy spots!" Stop this part of the program by suggesting that if people have any "spots" left over they can take them home and share them with members of their family.

If your group is large, divide the members into three smaller groups and assign the following questions. A smaller group could do this together. Provide large pieces of paper so that individual names can be written on separate papers and shared later.

Group 1   Identify a woman who has made a contribution in your church through her leadership and describe what she has done. Then, do the same for a woman in your community. What particular skills do these women possess?

Group 2	Name a woman theologian. Do you know this woman, or have you heard her speak? Maybe you have read something she has written. Describe your idea of a theologian.
Group 3	Name someone you consider a spiritual woman. Explain what you mean by spirituality. Are there spiritual women working in secular activities within our communities? Can you name one?

At the end of this exercise you should have the names of at least three or four women. Ask each group to give a brief comment about why they selected each particular woman. Hold up the papers individually and for each name written down have the group say: We affirm (name) for her contribution to (name of church, or name of community).

It would be very "affirming" if letters went to each of these women, describing your program, and indicating why you wish to recognize their contribution to church or community at this time.

Another suggestion is to think of someone within your congregation or community who is an "unsung heroine," someone who works quietly, yet seldom receives recognition. Is there some way that your group can recognize and affirm her?

To close, ask someone to join with you in this two-person commissioning:

One:	We have affirmed one another.
Two:	*We have proclaimed the names of other women...*

One:	Women who have contributed to our churches and communities
Two:	*through leadership and decision making, through theology and spirituality.*
One:	Let us go from here in strength and solidarity with women everywhere.
Two:	*Let us go challenged to use our talents and resources to respond to the call of Christ.*

SUMMER

Lay Education

WORSHIP

Call to Worship

If we believe in the "priesthood of all believers," we all share in Christ's ministry. By our baptism we belong to the holy catholic church, an organization filled with people who have gone into the world, making disciples, baptizing and teaching, confident always that their Lord and Saviour, Jesus Christ, was always with them. Let us worship God as revealed to us by that same Jesus.

Prayer

Gracious God, we thank you for witnesses throughout the years who have shared their faith with family and neighbours. We thank you for those ordained and commissioned, set apart by the church for special tasks. Especially, O God, we thank you for those whose service involved other forms of ministry: doctors, nurses, teachers, economists, farmers, homemakers, people in all walks of life, who have worked tirelessly, often unaware of the connection between their worship and work. Support all forms of ministry, we pray, and grant that together, lay and ordered ministers, we may ever seek to know and do your will. Amen.

Hymn
"We Have This Ministry" (#76 SGP)

Scripture
Matthew 28:16-20

REFLECTION

The closing words of Matthew's gospel are very familiar to us. Many of us have felt challenged by that great commission, that imperative of Jesus to "go therefore and make disciples of all nations; ..." (Mt. 28:19a) These are the words that inspired the great missionaries of the church. These are also the words that we are reconsidering as we enter the 21st century.

Can we assume that because, for us, Jesus is central to our faith, he must therefore be central to the faith of the whole world? There are other faith communities whose lives and beliefs we are gradually learning to respect, without negating in any way *our* faith in Jesus Christ. We all claim that there is one God — we are learning that it may be possible that God has been revealed to different people in different ways.

Although these words recorded in Matthew's gospel were directed to specific disciples, many other people took up the challenge. People like Paul and his followers. People like Stephen, and other martyrs of the Christian Church. In most of the very early Christian groups there was no distinction between ordained ministry and lay — Paul claimed that in Christ there is "... no longer slave or free, there is no longer male and female ..." (Gal. 3:28, in part.)

Lay people have always known and accepted that we are all one in Christ, yet the mystery of ordination and commissioning, the almost magical effect of the laying on of hands, has set ordered ministry apart in much more than function. Professional ministers have been at times put upon a pedestal. Over the centuries they have received special concessions from merchants and government, they have been revered by their congregations, and they have been expected to adhere to almost impossible moral standards.

Much of this is no longer true, and lay people are beginning to recognize their own valid ministry. They have discovered that a lay ministry cannot be exercised without including some knowledge of the Bible and some study of theology in their education.

Prayer

We pray for all who learn, for all who teach. We pray especially for those who teach and seek to learn knowledge of the Bible: for students in theological schools, for their professors and mentors, for lay people in Bible study groups and lay training courses, for all who seek to know your will and to do it. In the name of Jesus Christ we pray. Amen.

PROGRAM

The topic of this program is Lay Education, which essentially means education for lay *ministry*. We must not, however, assume that all of the people in our churches recognize their work (inside and/or outside the home) or their involvement within the church or community as a form of ministry. Discuss this concept, using as much affirmation as required to assure each person present that they *do* have a valid ministry, regardless of whether or not they name it as such.

If we were to prepare resumes for our lay ministry we might be surprised to discover how well we qualify. Have group members name courses they have taken, workshops they have attended, Bible Study groups and other forms of recognized lay training which they have experienced. Stress the fact that even though some of these courses may not have been very long, and probably did not qualify for university credits, they are still important facets of our training for ministry. If someone has taken an extended period of lay training, allow time for sharing some of that experience. (This would be an excellent time to promote a lay training centre in your area, or to advertise an upcoming opportunity for training.)

Now ask group members to name some *life experiences* that would qualify for their own ministerial resume. They will come up with things like Sunday School teaching, leadership positions in church committees, using their talents in the kitchen or the workshop. Bring out as many as you can, and remind them that visiting the sick, the lonely or the bereaved is ministry that can be done by lay people as well as those in paid ministry. Counselling can be the professional type, or it can be a listening ear to a neighbour with problems. Both are a form of ministry. Inviting a friend to church is a ministry of evangelism. Reading scripture, singing in the choir, or assisting with communion are all acts of the ministry of worship. You may wish to use a flip chart to list these areas of lay ministry, or just allow them to arise from your discussion.

As we seek to train ourselves for lay ministry, most of us discover that public prayer, even in small, familiar groups, is difficult. Depending on your group's experience in this area, it would be an excellent learning experience if members would close the program part of your time together with a circle prayer. (In a circle, holding hands, each person prays one sentence, usually beginning and ending with the leader.) Choose a particular topic for your prayer, such as the various aspects of ministry. Emphasize that taking part is not compulsory. Should someone not wish to participate, suggest that when their turn comes around they squeeze the hand of the person next to them, indicating a "pass." As you, the leader, close this circle of prayer include a prayer of thanks for the ministry of the members of your group.

SUMMER

Environment

WORSHIP

Call to Worship
Listen to one of God's promises to Isaiah: "... for I give water in the wilderness, rivers in the desert, to give drink to my chosen people, the people whom I formed for myself so that they might declare my praise." (Isa. 43:20b) Let us praise the God who spoke to Isaiah, who speaks to us.

Prayer
God of the rainbow promise, God of Isaiah and our God, we know that you desire a world of beauty for your people, a world full of resources for our well-being. We are sad that this earth is in danger, we are sad and we feel powerless. What can we do? Where do we start? Challenge us, O God, to renew our efforts to protect our environment, for ourselves, for our children, and for our children's children. Amen.

Hymn
"To Show by Touch and Word" (#134 SGP)

Scripture
  Isaiah 51:3 and 55:10-13

REFLECTION

Time and time again, throughout history, God has forgiven humans for the way we have refused to follow God's plan for creation, for the way we have treated one another, and the way we have treated the earth. The desert stories of the Bible record times when people's disobedience led them into deprivation and desolation. And yet, in the midst of any desert time, God holds out comfort and hope.

God wants us to choose to live in the garden of Eden — it is our own wilful nature that leads us into desert places. The circle continues, however, as God never gives up on us. The promise of our going out in joy, being led back in peace, mountains and trees rejoicing, and cypress and myrtle replacing thorns and brier, all of these things shall be "an everlasting sign that shall not be cut off."

Does this mean that we sit back and wait for God to rescue us, yet again? Or does it mean that there is still hope for our world if we see it as God's world, instead of ours?

The powerlessness we feel when faced with the immensity of the environmental challenge before us is understandable. Surely it is big business that is polluting our lakes and oceans with the discharges from their factories? Surely it is the advertising industry that insists that our food be over-packaged, so that the bright coloured pictures can tempt us to buy again? Why should we have to recycle our garbage when "they" are the problem? When we point a finger at "them" we need to remember that three of our fingers are pointing back at us.

Truth is, friends, that the story of the snowflakes works two ways. What snowflakes, you ask? Well, one single, beautiful, symmetrical snowflake is a wonder to behold. A few million of them give us that Christmas spirit and bring back memories of snow angels, snow balls, and warm cups of cocoa after our play. But many millions of these beautiful snowflakes can cause much harm. They cause traffic fatalities, heart attacks, they destroy tree branches and even provoke floods when they melt.

In the same manner, therefore, one person may feel that their insignificant amount of garbage is not contributing to the garbage disposal problem. But when multiplied by the millions of other people who discard the same insignificant amount, the result is a landfill site that can no longer be used. Then comes the wrangling that goes on in our communities when we try to find some way to dispose of everyone's "small" amount of garbage. Wouldn't it be better to assume that our individual efforts at reducing, reusing, and recycling, when compounded by more and more people getting in on the "3-R" act, would ultimately have a major influence on the garbage situation?

It is difficult for a community to maintain an interest in saving the environment. Children enjoy participating in environmental projects but after the project is done their candy bar wrapper often ends up in the gutter. What is needed is a change of attitude within the whole of our society. There is no better place to illustrate the power of people united for a cause than in a faith community. Here people share many of the same values, they teach those values to the children, and they can set excellent examples for the community at large. In times past, when churches were the tallest buildings in our cities, instead of banks, religion was powerful enough to influence the attitudes of society. Such influence is severely limited as we enter the 21st Century, but not yet entirely eroded. All of us as individuals can make an impact on our homes, our communities, and our earth.

Prayer

Unite us, dear God, in a crusade to promote loving care for our environment. Let us challenge one another to proclaim composting a form of worship, recycling an act of faith, and excess packaging an idol that we do not wish to honour. And please, we pray, do not give up on us, but let your word accomplish your own will for this earth. In Jesus name, Amen.

PROGRAM

We should not assume that because we have gathered as Christians that everyone present feels the same commitment to the environment. The "why?" questions are always the difficult ones: Why do we have to feel obligated to reduce, reuse, and recycle? Why should we write letters or otherwise protest when factories refuse to reduce the amount of pollution they create? The answers to the "why?" questions often determine our theology, just as our theology often determines the answers.

If your group is large enough, divide into three sections. Otherwise select one or two of the questions for the whole group to discuss.

Group 1   Read Genesis 1:27-30. What is your understanding of the word "dominion"? (Webster's Dictionary says that the word means "sovereignty, rule; territory of a government."[15] Dominion is related to God — how would God rule?)

Group 2   Read Genesis 9:8-17. Who does God include in this Covenant? (Noah *and every living creature*. Do you think that God would approve of over-fishing in the North Atlantic? If the rain forest and all its plants and animals are part of the Covenant, should our "dominion" allow us to destroy such areas?)

Group 3   Read 1 Corinthians 11:23-27. The new covenant was sealed with Jesus' blood. Blood is the symbol for life, in this case the life of Jesus himself. God gave God's own son to seal the Covenant made with all living things at Creation. The Covenant which began at Creation is therefore still in effect — sealed — because of the life, death and resurrection of Jesus. Does this help us answer the question "Why should I get involved in environmental issues?"

Close your time together by

- sharing some ways in which group members already reduce, reuse, and recycle,
- sharing some additional ways in which members could reduce, reuse, and recycle, i.e., using cloth napkins and bringing mugs to meetings when a lunch is served or providing receptacles for paper to be recycled,
- providing information about recycling depots, or programs.

Extra Resources

Starting from Scratch

With increased demands on women's time nowadays, preparing programs for use in church groups "from scratch" is difficult and often impossible. The twenty-three programs in this book can be used as presented, modified to suit your needs, or used as a starting point to create your own program. The impetus for creating a program for your group might be the desire to cover a theme that has not been covered before or to introduce one that is particularly relevant to your organization or community. New political developments throughout the world and new community forces at home make reflection and group discussion an important source of renewal. Exploring our spirituality in a changing world helps create the inner strength to deal with those changes.

Each program in this book is divided into three main sections — worship, reflection, and program — with common elements repeating from one to another. The worship section consists of a call to worship, scripture reading, hymn, and prayer (the latter three in any order which makes sense). The reflection is a short meditation, ending with a prayer, on the meaning of the worship section and ties it to the program or discussion section. The program section can involve group discussion and sharing stories, bible study, a guest speaker, brainstorming for ideas to implement in church work, or any other interactive means of working through the "theme" of the material.

The following outline will help you get started and can be filled out or altered and expanded as your ideas develop:

Worship
    Call to Worship
    Hymn
    Scripture
    Prayer
Reflection
    Meditation
    Prayer
Program
    Opening
    Discussion
    Closing
    Suggestions for Further Action or Reading

The following points can also help you get organized and get started:

1. Theme	Find a topic for your program, preferably related to the needs of your group.
2. Plan	You will need a general idea of what you're going to do, and how you expect to do it.
3. Advertise	Generate some enthusiasm through posters, announcements, word of mouth, etc.

4. Materials	Gather up whatever resources you can find, and any necessary equipment or "props."
5. Helpers	Decide who is going to take part in the program. (Those involved will benefit the most.)
6. Timing	Get an idea of how long your program will take by running through it with your helpers. Trim or expand where necessary.
7. Check	Check over the details one last time. Make sure the materials are gathered, the helpers are ready, the equipment is in place, etc.
8. Presentation	Present your program — and yes, you should be able to relax and enjoy yourself (this also helps others relax and enjoy themselves).
9. Evaluate	Let those who attend make you feel good but don't be afraid to accept some constructive criticism.
10. Follow Up	Suggest some specific action that could result from the program.

Two Carols for Advent

by Dorothy MacNeill

WHEN JOHN THE BAPTIST DID PROCLAIM

When John the Baptist did proclaim a greater One would come,
The people heard and were baptized with water, every one.
But one shall come, he told them, of whom the prophets spoke,
The Promised One, Messiah, to save all faithful folk.

He will baptize in Spirit, for He will be God's Son,
And all who hear and honour him will know He is the One —
The One to heal and comfort the One for all the world.
Make straight the highway then for Him, with banners now
    unfurled.

Until that blessed coming, the Advent we await,
We watch and pray and thus prepare our faith to truly state:
We will proclaim Christ's coming, we know him here and now,
And hope some day to see his face, and then before him bow.

(Melody: St. Louis, #421, HB)

ADVENT SEASON GIVES THE REASON

Advent season gives the reason
We prepare a special way.
Candles burning, children yearning,
Now's the time to watch and pray.
Strings are strumming, drums are drumming,
Voices humming, Christ is coming!
Soon it will be Christmas Day!
Soon it will be Christmas Day!

Advent greetings, special meetings,
See how fast the weeks go by!
We're preparing and we're sharing
To be ready, we will try.
Hope eternal, peace our passion,
Joy sustains us, Love's in fashion,
Soon we'll hear babe Jesus cry.
Soon we'll hear babe Jesus cry.

(Melody: Polish Carol, #63 *The Hymnary*)

Symbol of Hope

In - to the tem - ple the wid - ow came
Re - con - cil - ing love that flows
Thought-ful - ly laid a - side in prayer

Bear - ing her coin and sor - row.
Jus - tice that rolls like a riv - er.
Coins from the world we are shar - ing.

In - to the trea - sury her off - 'ring went
Peace that comes to a world of pain
Gath-ered, then shared in love and joy

Sym - bol of hope for to - mor - row.
Sym - bol of hope for the giv - er.
Sym - bol of hope for all liv - ing.

Original words and tune for International Committee for the Fellowship of the Least Coin (FLC). The FLC is an international movement of prayer for peace, justice, and reconciliation. By setting aside the least coin of her country as she prays, every women—rich or poor—may participate on an equal basis.

© Betty Radford Turcott, 1989.

Notes

Priscilla, Superwoman Model
[1] Cruden, *Cruden's Complete Concordance* , p. 514.
[2] Deen, *All of the Women of the Bible*, p. 230.

Mahala, the Ordinary
[3] Mahala Brace lived in Green's Harbour, Newfoundland, and was the author's grandmother.

Living Thanks
[4] A Prayer in common usage which may have originated with the Alcoholics Anonymous organization. Author unknown.

Being the Light
[5] Argus Poster © 1972. Text by Edith Wharton.
[6] *The Hymnary of the United Church of Canada*, # 613.

Beating the Blues
[7] *Good News Bible*, p. 724.
[8] Source unknown.

Stewardship
[9] Turcott, *Songs For The Journey*, p. 28.

Crocus Minded
[10] Carr and Sorely, *Bless This Mess & Other Prayers*, p. 14.
[11] *Ibid.*, p. 16.

Christ's Body, the Church
[12] Anglican Church of Canada, *The Book of Common Prayer*, p. 39.
[13] *A Place For You* , p. 28.
[14] *The Avery & Marsh Song Book*, p. 32.

Environment
[15] *Webster's Dictionary*, p. 127.

BIBLIOGRAPHY

Anglican Church of Canada, The *Book of Common Prayer* (Cambridge: Cambridge University Press, 1962).

A Place For You (Toronto: Division of Mission in Canada, The United Church of Canada, 1989).

Carr, Jo, and Imogene Sorley, *Bless This Mess & Other Prayers* (Nashville, Tenn.: Abingdon Press, 1969).

Cruden, Alexander, *Cruden's Complete Concordance to the Old and New Testaments* (London: Lutterworth Press, 1951).

Deen, Edith, *All of the Women of the Bible* (New York: Harper and Row, 1955).

Faith in My Neighbour (Toronto: The United Church Publishing House, 1994).

Gibran, Kahlil, *The Prophet* (New York: Alfred A. Knopf, 1985).

Good News Bible (Toronto: Canadian Bible Society, 1976).

Holy Bible, New Revised Standard Version (Grand Rapids, Mich.: Zondervan Publishing House, 1989).

Lindburgh, Anne Morrow, *Gift from the Sea* (New York: Random House, 1991).

Newsom, Carol A., and Sharon H. Ringe, eds. *The Women's Bible Commentary* (Louisville, Ky.: Westminster/John Knox Press, 1992).

Nordtvedt, Matilda, and Pearl Steinkeehler, *Women's Programs for Every Season* (Chicago: Moody Press, 1982).

Reid, Clyde, *You Can Choose Christmas* (Waco, Tex.: Word Books, 1975).

Songs for a Gospel People (Winfield, B.C.: Wood Lake Books, 1988).

The Avery & Marsh Song Book (Port Jervis, N.Y.: Reclamation Productions, 1973).

The Holy Bible, King James Version (Cleveland and New York: The World Publishing Company).

The Hymn Book of the Anglican Church of Canada and the United Church of Canada (Toronto: Cooper & Beatty, 1971).

The Hymnary of the United Church of Canada (Toronto: The United Church Publishing House, 1930).

Turcott, Betty Radford, *Songs For The Journey* (Toronto: Women's Inter-Church Council of Canada, 1993).

Webster's Dictionary, New Compact Format (Larchmont, N.Y.: Book Essentials Press, 1969).

Index of Scripture Passages

NOTES